The Toxic Boss Babe

The Toxic Boss Babe

My Inside Story Of The Cult World Of Multi-Level Marketing And Escape From The Dark Side Of Forced Positivity.

A Memoir

LINDA CARROLL

◆ tributary

Published in Great Britain in 2025 by Tributary, an imprint of
Foreshore Publishing Limited
86-90 Paul Street London EC2A 4NE
www.foreshorepublishing.com
Reg. No. 13358650

ISBN: 978-1-0684467-0-2

A catalogue record for this book is available from the British Library

Printed and bound in UK.

Typeset in Adobe Garamond Pro Regular and Roboto by Richard Powell

To my sister Daniela, because of your amazing reaction
when I told you this book was happening.
To my Husband Jeff, my biggest supporter,
my rock and best friend.

cult noun
/kʌlt/

1. an extreme religious group that is not part of an established religion
2. a fashionable belief, idea, or attitude that influences people's lives

LONGMAN DICTIONARY OF CONTEMPORARY ENGLISH ONLINE

Definition of a cult: "A relatively small group of people having beliefs or practices regarded by others as strange or sinister, or as exercising excessive control over members,"

HUMAN RIGHTS RESEARCH CENTER

toxic adjective
/ˈtɒksɪk $ ˈtɑːk-/

1. containing poison, or caused by poisonous substances toxic chemicals/substances/fumes/gases
2. very unpleasant and causing a lot of harm or unhappiness

LONGMAN DICTIONARY OF CONTEMPORARY ENGLISH ONLINE

Prologue
2019

Do you want to work from home? Are you sick of working for someone else? Do you want to be your own boss? Do you want financial freedom? Do you want a job that will change your life? These were some of the many questions posed to me when I was first introduced to Multi-Level-Marketing. Hard to believe perhaps, however I had never heard of an MLM nor Pyramid Scheme – I know, you're probably thinking "really?!" – however I can say hand on heart, that I am telling the truth. The world of Network Marketing was a concept never introduced to me and something I was totally unaware of. This is the main reason for me writing this book – to hopefully warn others about the dangers of getting involved in this toxic world. Years ago, before the age of social media, the MLM rep would knock on your door, and I guess something like this was a lot easier to avoid. Nowadays however, MLM's recruit through social media – which exposes a far greater number of people. The company I got involved with currently has over a million representatives worldwide and no doubt this is growing day by day.

If a stranger had approached me asking me the above questions, I would have politely declined and carried on walking. I would have brushed it off as a scam. However, in my case, a trusted member of my family told me that she was living a life of total freedom, that she was her own boss and was earning approximately £2,000 a month and that I could achieve the same thing, why would I not believe them? After all, why would she lie to a member of her family or con me – you would assume that family looks out for each other, would never invite them to do or join in with something harmful or dodgy. I personally would fear the repercussions. I was born in the UK, my family is Italian, Italians, as I am sure many other nationalities do, pride themselves on strong family ties, it is absolutely unheard of to betray a member of your family. Therefore, when I was introduced

1

to this "business", I trusted this particular family member was being honest with me and had my best interests at heart. You may call it naivety, and you may be right. I just trusted someone I thought was a friend.

This book is based on my experience within a Multi-Level-Marketing business – one which, thank goodness was short lived, however a painful lesson none the less. It was an experience which deeply affected me, more so than I have let onto family and friends, it is an experience I still think about from time to time, due to the fact that it has shaped me into the person I am now. Five years on and I still think about what happened and yes, I still feel like a fool. It sadly has made me a lot more wary and mistrusting of strangers, as well as people I know. I am a lot more sceptical now also, however on a positive note, it has made me stronger in character and a lot more confident. I hope that through this book, I will warn others away from Multi-Level-Marketing or at least convince people to fully research into it before making any final commitment. This book may also help people who have been affected to talk about their experiences truthfully with others, as I know there are many people involved who are too afraid to speak out or, sadly too embarrassed. I strongly believe this is why there are so many people unaware of the pitfalls of Multi-Level-Marketing, because no one is willing to truthfully talk about their experience.

I wrote a short blog about my MLM experience last year shortly after I left the "business", and as I received praise from people, strangers as well as friends and family for my bravery in telling the truth about such schemes, I decided to elaborate more. In this book, I have of course changed the names of the people involved and have used a different name for the company I was associated with, and I reiterate once again that this is *my* experience of the MLM company I was involved with. I am sure that many people will read this and leap to the defence of the Companies they are involved with, more for the fact that if they were to speak the truth, they will lose the people below them in their pyramid scheme and through this, their income. This being said, remember that those at the top of the pyramid (The Boss Babes) are the ones earning from the misfortune of those on the lower levels and they will praise the "business" as being the best thing that ever happened to them. You will of course make up your own minds and if you, like me, are going through the same thoughts and feelings and can see your money trickling away with no view of the so call success your being promised – by one hundred percent honest with yourself and stop. Just stop and really think about what you're doing and why you're doing it. The one thing I want you to take away from this is that you're not a failure and that it's okay to quit. I did and it was the best decision I made – I finally felt free.

Chapter 1

Let me begin with a little bit about me and how I ended up being "My Own Boss". I was born in Islington, North London and lived in the same area until 2018 when my husband and I wanted to escape the "Big Smoke" so to speak and move out of town to somewhere a little more rural, however not too far away as I still needed to commute to my job which was, at the time based in London.

We decided upon a town in Hertfordshire, it was perfectly placed – a mere twenty-five minutes by train into London Kings Cross and my brother-in-law had been living in the area for years and my husband and I became fond of the town after we first visited him when he moved there.

I was working as an Administrator for a private nursery school in their head office and had been part of the team there for just over four years. I had a good relationship with my colleagues and employer, and although I liked working there, the role had become a little stale and there was no real way for me to progress up the career ladder. I envisaged going into my forties, still stuck in the same job, doing the same thing day in and day out and so I began a rather half-hearted attempt in looking for a role elsewhere. I was uncertain as to what I wanted to do; however, I knew I didn't want to be stuck in yet another administrative role.

My husband and I are child free by choice and without the responsibility of having to think about pulling a child or children out of school and away from friends etc, we decided to up sticks. We sold our flat in North London and moved to Hertfordshire in July 2018. We were (and still are) very happy, and although I knew no one in the small town, except for my husband of course and his brother, I was content as my family and friends were all just a hop, skip and a train journey away.

One afternoon in October that same year, my mother came to visit and she mentioned that her cousin who I had not seen in years lived close by in the same town. I was actually pleased as I had happy memories of playing at my great aunt and uncles house as a child and my cousin, who is a lot older than me, was actually a really nice man, I had a good relationship with him and with all of his brothers (five of them in total), so when on a Saturday evening in November, my cousin Paul turned up unannounced at my house with his wife Julia, whom I had never met – I was surprised and really pleased to see him again.

He had changed a lot, due to having aged over the years obviously, however it was as if it were only yesterday that I had last seem him and the conversation flowed easily and it was great to catch up on the family news. His wife was lovely, and we talked about her daughter, from her previous marriage who was only ten years my junior. Paul was happy that we now lived locally and was keen to invite my husband and I to his house for dinner and drinks as soon as possible, in fact the next evening. He promised that his other brother, Frances would be there, as well as Sarah, Julia's daughter. My husband and I agreed to the impromptu invitation, swept up in having found more family ties in the area and we arranged to be at their house for dinner on the following evening.

My younger sister Danni was also at my house the evening when Paul and Julia visited and already knew Julia's daughter, having met her when they were teenagers, Danni used to visit Paul and Julia for sleep overs with Sarah which I vaguely remembered. Danni declined the invite on Sunday and when Paul and Julia left, she confided in me that she and Sarah had fallen out, due to "boy troubles" - apparently a boy who Sarah liked, had actually preferred my sister and Sarah had warned Danni to back off.

It was nothing serious, however Sarah's behaviour had deterred Danni from rekindling their friendship and they simply drifted apart. I put this down to a teenage quarrel and thought no more of it. I had never met Sarah and didn't think it was fair to judge her on something which happened between her and my sister years ago. James and I were looking forward to our mini family reunion.

Chapter 2

The next evening as promised, my husband and I arrived at Paul and Julia's house, a mere ten-minute drive away from our home and was warmly greeted by Frances, his new wife – whom I had never met and Sarah and her husband Max who both seemed really nice. Sarah seemed initially to be a little "stand offish" and curled up on the sofa at the back of the living room, engrossed with her phone. Once the food was laid out, the various conversations were flowing and it actually turned out to be a really nice evening.

Sarah and I chatted away about various things, she asked me about what sort of job I was doing, about life in London before our move and the various destinations my husband and I had travelled to around the world.

Sarah and I were both Instagram users and "befriended" one and other on the app that evening, and while we were chatting, Sarah had a quick look at my profile and noticed that I had posted pictures of beauty products on my page.

I wasn't selling or promoting the brands, I simply posted about products I purchased and used because I liked them. I absolutely love all things beauty and skincare related and pride myself on investing in high quality products. I enjoyed posted about the products and I viewed it as a little lifestyle hobby, nothing more. I didn't view myself as an "Influencer", nor was I paid to advertise for companies, I did it purely for fun. I didn't look at Sarah's page, however she commented that we did the same thing and that we had similar interests. She said no more and although I tried to go back to the subject once or twice, I was unable to find out more about what she did, she simply mentioned owning her own business and as we had just met, I felt it would be perhaps rude to pry too much, the last think I wanted was for her to think I was being nosey.

It was getting late, James and I had work to get up for early the next day therefore we said our goodbyes and Sarah and I promised to keep in touch. It was nice knowing that there was yet another family member I could now add to my Hertfordshire list. On my way to work the next day, I thought I would kill a few minutes of my train commute by looking at Sarah's Instagram page. It was a pleasant surprise to see her posts about beauty, her page was actually really nice, her posts were well presented and I was becoming more and more intrigued about this "business" which she never really elaborated on when we met the previous evening. Her posts were quite cryptic, if and when she posted about a product, unlike me where I would openly show the brand and disclose the name of what I was using and posting about, Sarah's posts never gave any real details – only that she was using this "amazing clay mask" or "amazing facial cleansing devise", while strategically placing her finger over the name or logo.

I couldn't understand why all the secrecy? One post that did intrigue me mentioned a "Business Opportunity" and that she was looking to introduce five trusted people to this "Amazing" business. She promised financial freedom, working from home, being your own boss, in fact she was a Company Director of her very own beauty business. Sarah looked really happy and what with feeling a little deflated with my work life at the time, I admit I was curious. It was not long before I messaged Sarah asking her for more information about her "Business", I mentioned that I wanted to learn more and was genuinely interested, especially seeing as it revolved around beauty. It didn't take long before I received a reply back and she said it would be best to speak over the phone. We agreed for me to call her the next evening on my way home from the train station. Unbeknown to me, I had fallen for the first part of the scam, hook, line and sinker.

Chapter 3

I called Sarah as promised on my walk home, we had not spoken since our first meeting at my cousins and it was nice to hear from her. We exchanged pleasantries and she asked me how my day had been. I explained it had been a typical day in the office and she commented on how she couldn't bear the thought of commuting into London, how she didn't envy me and that she was so grateful to have the flexibility and convenience to be able work from home. At this stage I was really keen to learn more about her business, however Sarah always seemed to navigate away from telling me directly about what she did. She asked me why I was unhappy in my job, why I liked the beauty industry, what I was looking for financially, I noticed how after every reply, her response was "God, yeah, just like me", "Oh my God you're perfect for this", "This is gonna be *amazing* for you".

Telling Sarah about my woes felt as if I was speaking to a therapist, unloading my problems onto her and wanting to find a magic solution to everything. Sarah mentioned that when she first looked at my Instagram page, she was convinced I was already doing the same thing. Sarah explained that she did what I did i.e. posting about products, yet she got paid for it. She asked me why I promoted other people's products for free? She also asked me if I was open minded about using a brand that was not stocked in shops and if I was a "Product Snob". I said I was open to using anything, as long as it was good quality. She then told me her life story, how and why she got into the "business", about all the friends she had made on the journey, where she envisaged herself in five years' time. She spoke openly to me about some traumatising experiences she had had and how the "business" had seen her though some dark times.

I admit, I loved the energy and good vibes I experienced during the conversation. Although she was taking about bad experiences, it had been the business she was now in that had changed her life for the better. She mentioned that she previously worked in a call centre, but hated her dead-end job and that after just two years working the "business" she was able to leave her full-time job as she was now earning the salary equivalent working from home. The more and more she spoke, the more curious I became.

She explained that the next step for me would be to come along to a group meeting as her guest. She could not contain her excitement at the fact that the following Wednesday's meeting was a special one, as there was going to be a guest speaker there, a woman who had been working the "business" for just five years and was already earning £19,000 a month. I made Sarah repeat this several times, as I simply could not comprehend what she was saying. Again, £19,000 a month seemed like a ridiculous amount of money – I was gobsmacked.

I even scoffed a little when she repeated the amount, to which Sarah replied that she had no reason to lie to me, we were, technically family, why would she lie to me knowing that if found out, it could ruin our relationship, and that my cousin Paul's would be really upset if he found out.

She had a point, I mean, why lie? She was my cousins step daughter, if she was lying, surely, he would be none too pleased to know that she was behaving this way towards me, especially seeing as Paul and I got on so well. I agreed to go along to the meeting the following Wednesday after work. This could be the new career change I had been waiting for! After our phone conversation, Sarah and I messaged frequently throughout the week and into the next. We commented and liked each other's Instagram posts and I felt we were developing a really nice relationship. I could not believe how much she had confided in me and the fact that she was sharing this business opportunity with me. I was happy also to have made a new friend who lived close to home. I want to repeat again that I had never heard of Multi-Level-Marketing Companies, I was also quite new to social media and only used Instagram – I was a novice really and I guess naïve to the dark side of social media.

Chapter 4

Sarah happily agreed to collect me at the station in the town centre where I lived, in order to drive to the hotel in St Albans where the meeting was taking place. I noticed as I approached her car that Sarah had another girl with her, apparently, she too had been doing this "business" a little while ago, but stopped for a few months and was now wanting to get back into it. On the drive to the hotel, Sarah spoke about Anna, the £19,000 a month earner, about how amazing she was and how one day it would be her giving motivational talks to people at meetings.

I asked Sarah how long she had been involved in the "business" and she said it was coming up to four years, however due to the difficult times she had had, she had not always been as dedicated as she should have been. She was rectifying this now and was going to throw herself into it one hundred percent. We arrived at the hotel and I was surprised to see quite a crowd already congregating in the lobby. We were in one of the conference rooms upstairs and as Sarah was in charge of ticking names off of the attendance list, we headed upstairs. The seating in the room was arranged in rows, with a large screen at the front. The majority of the women attending were quite young and I admit, I did feel a little bit out of place, however Sarah reassured me that this was just the tip of the iceberg and that the "Business" had thousands of "members" of all different age groups, male and female.

As I looked for a seat, Sarah introduced me to a couple of the other girls there who were polite. I mentally chided myself for not

11

refreshing my makeup before leaving work. The girls were almost looking through me, not at me and their smiles didn't quite reach their eyes. I had come straight from the office, was wearing my work clothes, I hadn't had time glam up and was wearing what I usually wore, very little makeup. I tried not to let my insecurities get the better of me and sat down ready to listen to the presentation.

The meeting organiser took her place by a large television screen and welcomed everyone, she then asked us to give a warm welcome to the guest speaker, "A women who is literally smashing this business – a real Boss Babe - Anna!" A young woman in her twenties walked into the room and stood by the screen. She wore a very loose leopard print tunic top over wet look leggings and thigh high boots. Anna began by talking about her life, it was a real rag to riches story, how she too had started off working in a call centre on a low wage with no job prospects. She was "tired of being tired" and hating the fact that life was passing her by, bearing in mind she was in her early twenties, I thought that sentence was a little over dramatic.

Anna explained how she was sick of earning money for someone else, whilst she was constantly broke. She had a toddler and husband and wanted a better future for them. So far, so good. I could see where she was coming from and I guess I too wanted better for myself. She became quite passionate throughout her talk, asking us all what we wanted from life. Did we just want to get up and go to work on the tube, train etc…scraping by in a job we hate, making money for someone else, or did we want more from life. She made it sound like having a 9-5, Monday to Friday job should be something to be ashamed of, working for someone else was a bad thing, and that you hadn't really achieved anything in life if you did this.

Anna then went on to explain that she decided one day, upon seeing a "business" opportunity online that she was going to take a risk and go for it, "you only live once" she said, "be your own boss, be a Boss Babe", at this I did cringe a little, however more and more of what she said appealed to me. Who wouldn't want to be their own boss, work from home, not have to commute, choose your own hours of work, when you took time off, earn money in your sleep (yes, once again you read correctly). All of this Sarah, Anna and many more were doing and Sarah was offering me this gift (her words), as I was technically family.

Anna then bragged that she was now on £19,000 a month, after only five years in the business. She had retired her husband who now stayed at home with her, supporting her in the running on her empire. A couple of photos on the screen showed Anna standing in front of a nice car, expensive by the look of it, of her standing in a nice, large kitchen in a very modern house. She looked happy, confident, and pleased with her life.

During the next part of the meeting, Anna showed us a presentation which explained who the company was that we would be partnered with. I had never heard of them - TrueVisage an American Company which had been founded back in the eighties. The PowerPoint presentation showed some of the products, I admit, my heart sunk a little at the look of the packaging, it was absolutely not the sort of thing I would buy. It looked dated and a little cheap, however I was determined not to be the "Product Snob" Sarah mentioned on our first call. I wanted to keep an open mind, I mean, Anna was raking in £19k a month, right? The products must be good? Sarah mentioned other girls who were partnered with TrueVisage who were huge successes. She provided me with a list of names and recommended I should begin to follow them immediately on Instagram, they too were doing really well and making lots of money.

The slides kept on coming, some of which explained the business structure and payment and which were a little complicated. Anna drilled it into us that we wouldn't work directly for TrueVisage, nor be paid a wage by them. We would be our own bosses and earn commission based upon sales and sign-ups. There were various stages you needed to get to in order to earn pin titles and reward trips, which sounded great. I was still unsure as to how I would make the equivalent of my own current salary, let alone the figures some of the top earners were making just by promoting products on social media and selling products, I mean the mark-up was quite high, but still, I would have to sell a huge amount, therefore was I missing something?

Chapter 5

Anna moved onto the introduction phase, or "recruitment" process. The top cash was earned by introducing people to the business. Signing someone up as a "Downline", which would in turn, make you their "Upline". Every time your Downline purchased a product you immediately earned a commission. This was on top of your own direct sales, and your own purchases of course. Now remember, I had never heard of Multi-Level Marketing or Pyramid Schemes, I simply viewed this as group business model, a kind of team business.

The recruitment stage was sold to us by TrueVisage in a way so that it felt like we were doing every sign up a favour, giving them the gift of financial freedom. We were told that the best way to start out was to approach friends and family members, as they would jump at the chance to support you in your new business venture. Anna became deadly serious at this point regarding the fact that friends who didn't support you, well, they obviously weren't your true friends. If family members choose not to support you, well, that says it all really – they were obviously jealous. The room became quiet and Anna shrugged her shoulders and said "the truth hurts, but I learned the hard way. My circle got smaller, but my vision and dreams got bigger". Anna told us that we needed to convince our nearest and dearest to sign up so that they could purchase the products with up to a forty percent discount using their own wholesale account, as opposed to buying direct from you – you were practically doing *them* a favour and still making money in the process!

I admit, I did find the business model a little bit complicated, the various stages of recruitment, and how many people to recruit in order to gain certain pin titles and awards and I was a little bamboozled by it all at first, however I was confident that Sarah could explain it in a simpler way to me at a later stage. I also accepted that this wasn't a get rich quick business, like any other business, it was going to take time. During the last part of the meeting we heard true testimonials from some of the other attendees. Why they had adopted the "Business" and at what stage they were at. Some of the women were just starting out, there was also one man there, which I must admit, did surprise me, however he thought the business model was good. He worked as a manager in sales and seemed to know what he was talking about, which was reassuring.

Everyone in the room seemed to me to be mature and sensible, yes words such as "Boss Babe" did crop up from time to time, however this was more from the much younger girls and I guess the majority of the time, some of them were trying to appeal to the younger crowd. Everyone seemed savvy and sensible. There were a few others, who had been working their businesses for quite a while now and were hopeful to one day be quitting their full-time jobs to make this a full-time business. The ultimate message was positivity. Anna explained that before TrueVisage found her (yes, this was also a popular phrase – TrueVisage finds you, you don't find TrueVisage) she was miserable, surrounded by negative people and constantly moaning about life. Now, she was forever grateful, positive and surrounded by like-minded people, who shared the same vision. Positivity and a positive mindset was really pushed around in this circle, it was all about being positive and I know now, through this experience the difference between simply being positive in a natural, organic sense and the toxic positivity which is rammed down your throat when you are involved with an MLM.

Anna, Chloe (who I later found out was Sarah's Upline, and technically my Upline also as we were in the same pyramid) and Sarah were the only ones at the meeting running their "businesses" full time. I met Chloe, who just like some of the others that evening, didn't really acknowledge me – I was way too plain (and probably old) for her – most of the girls there were in the late teens and twenties. I was thirty-eight, soon to be thirty-nine.

I didn't take it to heart too much, Sarah had invited me and was offering me the chance to start my own beauty business and after

Anna's presentation, I felt confident and happy I belonged there also. Overall, it had been a good evening and I was feeling really positive (the organic sense…). Most of what was said I agreed with and I felt a huge sense of belonging. We were all looking for something better. We all wanted to improve our lives and this really did seem like a great way to do it. It was eventually time to leave, Sarah of course dropped me off home, asked me how I felt and if I was interested. At this stage, I was happy to buy one or two of the products, just to see what they were like. Sarah was pleased and said she would send me her TrueVisage UK ID number so that I could open up my free wholesale business account, linked to her, therefore she would be my official Upline and I could order products to begin using and promoting. She assured me that orders would flood through in no time!

Chapter 6

When I arrived home, James asked me how the meeting went, I explained it all to him as best as I could and told him about Anna, earning £19,000 a month. He too baulked at this and I assured him just as Sarah did with me that it was true, after all Sarah told me she wouldn't lie. I also told him about Chloe, Sarah's Upline, who was earning roughly the same. My husband is an amazing man and I trust him one hundred percent and know that whenever he advises me about anything, he does so with my best interests at heart. He is eighteen years my senior and is incredibly "life educated" and immediately told me to be careful, that this all sounded like a Pyramid Scheme.

I wish I had listened to him looking back now, I really do, however a combination of stubbornness, the fact that I was ready to leave a job which no longer made me happy and the fact that I looked at Sarah's life on Instagram (believing stupidly, no, I should correct that, naively that social media is a true portrayal of someone's life…I know, I know…but I'm being honest here….) and wanted the same thing, I was totally naïve and I guess I wanted to make new friends close to home. I laughed off his warning and I said I would take it slow and simply order a couple of products using my soon to be Wholesale Business Account.

The next day at work, with James's warning ringing in my ears I typed TrueVisage into the search engine on my computer. I guess a little research wouldn't hurt, just to be sure it was all legitimate. An array of articles and webpages popped up, most of which I was pleased to find were positive. I also searched and added the list of names which Sarah had provided me with on my Instagram and was impressed all of these super confident, successful women, "living life on their terms", working from home, surrounded by beautiful things and in gorgeous homes. Trus Boss Babes, living their best lives.

There were a few not so great articles, however I was determined not to be swayed by someone else's negative opinion and wanted to make up my own mind. I also think looking back that I read and accepted what *I* wanted to at the time. I was determined to do this, therefore was blinded to any negative reviews. You only see what you want to see as the saying goes.

Sarah's email came through just before my lunch break with all of the information I required to set up my free wholesale account. As soon as I was on my lunch break, I logged on, set up my account and placed my order, which was easier said than done. I accessed the TrueVisage website and clicked on the products tab and was a bit surprised that it simply provided a list of various product names, under various titles which meant nothing to me.

I didn't really know what I was looking for and it wasn't the easiest site to navigate. I message Sarah asking her which two products she would recommend, and she immediately pinged back a response "go for the Whitening Toothpaste and Mud Mask – both products are *amazing* and my best sellers!"

I was happy with this, after all, I didn't have a mud mask at home and tooth paste is always needed, I remember Anna boasting about both products at the St Albans meeting being her best sellers also. I had problems locating them on the website, there was no search bar and bizarrely, the products weren't simply called toothpaste or mud mask. Eventually with Sarah's detailed name descriptions I found them. I was surprised to see that the toothpaste was £12 and the Mud Mask was £30. I would spend around £2 - £4 on toothpaste (well-known brands), so I did think the price was a little bit steep.

I fired off a quick message to Sarah voicing my concerns over the prices. She immediately replied that this was the retail price, once I opened my wholesale account, I would be able to purchase the toothpaste with the forty percent discount, still this was nearly £7. Sarah once again messaged me stating that my business needed to be invested in. I technically had no overheads, no staff to pay, no packaging or production costs, think about all the money I would earn if I just invested a little now. She was right, I shouldn't moan, this was an investment into my business, if I start quibbling a few pounds now, I would get nowhere. Speculate to accumulate right? I did however resent the £6 postage cost but thought this no doubt meant that the products would be sent registered post and packaged beautifully!

Chapter 7

I waited patiently for my order and what would be the start to my business. Delivery took 3-5 working days. I was so excited by the prospect that this could be the start of my new career. During this time Sarah stayed in contact with me daily. It was nice to hear from her and it felt like she was nurturing me ready for my new business adventure. She also mentioned the exciting news about the up and coming Success Summit after Christmas, which was being held in London in January. This was a huge, two-day event, hosted on a Saturday and Sunday. Thousands were expected to attend, all of which were in the business or thinking of starting their own successful beauty business. Sarah said it was paramount for me to attend, this was going to be "life changing" for me, and I would learn so much. The ticket price was £50, once again I needed to view this as a business investment. When I told James, he said that usually companies paid for you to attend training days, why did I need to cough up £50? I explained that I was my own boss and that any conference costs needed to be paid for by me and/or my business. I didn't work for TrueVisage, however I did need to attend their events. Even now I can't believe I didn't question this and just accepted it.

I agreed that of course I would go. Sarah asked if I wanted to stay in the hotel with her, as she didn't see the point in travelling to and from London on both days. Luckily for me, I could stay at my parents for free which was a short taxi trip or bus ride from the hotel where the Success Summit was being held. I was filled with excitement for the New Year and what was to come. My new products eventually arrived and I couldn't hide my disappointment when they did.

The box had seen better days, however I guessed this was more the courier's fault than TrueVisage's. However, upon opening the box I was met with a cheap looking tube of mud clay in a murky blue coloured bottle, the logo and packaging was bland and the toothpaste, was well, just toothpaste – no real thought to product design or branding, the products certainly didn't look like they were worth £42 collectively!

Before TrueVisage, I would order the majority of my products from a well know, high-end High-Street Beauty stockist. The prices for products varied from £5-£10 up to £400 plus (note: I didn't spend that much – this is just to provide a guide as to product price!), however upon delivery you are greeted with a beautifully packaged, sleek box, products carefully wrapped in tissue paper, and you also receive a thank you gift of various beauty samples. The ingredients within the products are of a high quality. It was as if TrueVisage, founded in the eighties, was still well and truly stuck there. Once again, just as I did over the course of my time in the business, I made excuses which I tried to disguise as part and parcel of making my business work. I pulled my shoulders back and convinced myself that it was the actually product and how it performed that counted, not the packaging. Be positive!!

James and I were off on our Christmas holiday to Thailand, and I was going to take the products with me to post about them whilst away. I didn't want to blurt out on my social media just yet what my plans were in terms of starting my own beauty business and wanted to go away, focus on my holiday and make a fresh start upon my return – New Year, New Me, New Career!

Chapter 8

I was so sure this was what I wanted to do, that after the initial meeting in St Albans, after all of the messaging with Sarah and chats over the phone and looking at all the other women on Instagram and watching their "story" posts, I made the bold decision to quit my job just before Christmas. I wanted to throw myself into my new Beauty Business full time, dedicate myself to it one hundred percent. Looking back now this was obviously an incredibly rash decision (what some might call stupid and I guess rightly so). I hadn't properly research anything, I was relying on the honesty of a member of my family and trusting the people I had met. I was desperate to leave my office job and thought this was a "sign". At the meeting, Anna kept on touching upon the fact that "you don't find this business, this business finds you". I really did believe that everything happens for a reason, it was something Sarah also repeated on many occasions.

James agreed that I could use some of our savings to keep me going until my business took off. He was hugely supportive and he could tell this was important to me. I knew deep down he had his reservations, however being the wonderful, supportive husband that he is, he just wanted me to be happy and continued to champion my efforts with encouragement and support.

I was due to work my last day in the office in mid-January, my last day was in fact the week before the Success Summit (another "sign"). James and I had a wonderful holiday as always in Thailand, and I used my time lounging by the pool to read up on branding my business and potential business card designs. I was determined to do this properly and I wanted to be as professional as possible.

I chose a name for my business, as although we were selling the TrueVisage products, we were not working for them directly. TrueVisage were not paying me wages and I wasn't allowed to use their name directly under my business, therefore I named my business "Linda Beauty" and proudly named myself as Director. Looking back now I absolutely cringe at how stupid this all was, however I truly believed everything the TrueVisage representative told me, as they were also a direct line to Sarah and I knew she wouldn't dupe me. This all meant something, I was the Director of my own business, I represented Linda Beauty, however I sold TrueVisage products and represented their brand.

I took a photo of the Mud Mask and Toothpaste whilst away, uploading my usual posts about new products I was trialling out and was super impressed with. I didn't mention that I was selling the products. It was a natural post, used to gauge any comments I would receive. The mud mask was actually okay, it was a basic clay mask and did the trick, however there were much better brands on the market that basically did the same thing as a fraction of the price and this product didn't look like it was worth £30. I had concerns about how I was going to sell these items but put these to the back of my mind and implemented a positive mindset to convince myself it was great and everything would be fine.

When I returned from our Christmas break, I arranged for my business cards to be designed, I invested in some beautiful plain white boxes and lovely pink and grey (my brand colours) tissue paper, as when my orders started to flood in, I wanted to be able to dispatch the products in my own, branded boxes. We were unable to arrange for products to be dispatched directly from TrueVisage to customers, and judging on the look of the packaging I had received from TrueVisage, I preferred to repackage the items as I thought it would look better. TrueVisage would post the order to us and we then took the responsibility to distribute to our customers. It was a bit long winded, as it meant that if someone placed at order directly with me, it could take up to two weeks before they received it. As I would be repackaging the items, I toyed with the idea of enclosing little treats and asked Sarah about how we went about providing product samples.

Sarah explained that TrueVisage didn't supply product samples. I was confused, how was I supposed to let my customers try products first before committing to the high prices? I knew full well that the people I knew, such as my sister would want a sample first. The trick to this explained Sarah, was to purchase my own sample pots, and squeeze some of my own product into them to give away. I immediately thought that this would be quite limiting as so far, I only have the mask and the toothpaste. I would need to buy a few more products, perhaps a moisturiser, facial wash and body cream just in case. Plain pots would be a problem, however I quickly thought about buying little labels so that I could name the sample, this I suppose would have to do. I wasn't keen on the hygiene aspect of the process but had to work with what I was given. Again, I was told to be positive and all would be well.

Sarah was always helpful, guiding me in which products were popular, she was there to help me all the way, messaging me several times a day. She explained that at the Success Summit I would have the chance to see more of the products and try some for myself which would help me when ordering. The tricky part was that if customers asked me about products and how they performed, how would I know what to tell them, not having tried them all. Sarah mentioned that all would be explained at the Summit, especially on Sunday as this was the day for everyone interested about the business to gain key, insider tips on how to make your business successful. I really didn't know what to expect, however judging by the buzz on Instagram amongst all of the women currently working the business, it was set to be a great weekend. It had only been a short time however I already felt part of something good.

Chapter 9

It was the day of the Success Summit and I had arranged to meet Sarah at the hotel in Westminster, London at 10am. She would be there early as she had volunteered to be part of the set-up team. I dropped off my over-night bag at mum and dads and took a taxi as I didn't want to risk being late. As the taxi pulled up outside, I could already see quite a large group of people milling about outside and inside the foyer. I could tell that they were all here for the TrueVisage event. The vast majority of the women were seriously glammed up, full on makeup, hair extensions, nail extensions, lash extensions – the works.

I admit I once again felt out of place, I was wearing jeans, a cashmere sweater and a pair of ballet pumps, my makeup was as always, minimal. I also felt awkward as I knew nobody there. I couldn't see Sarah anywhere and managed to find my way downstairs into the basement area, where the conference room was based. There was no mobile phone reception at this level and I had no idea how Sarah and I would contact each other. I waited by the entrance, hoping she would eventually find me. Whilst I waited, I scoped out the room. There was a mix of people congregated together, you had the super glam squad, women who were so glammed up you would have thought they were attending a party, not an eyebrow hair out of place. The contrast in who was there surprised me the most, as although you had the glam squad type, you also had women there you looked painfully shy and awkward and plainly dressed (not a criticism!) The noise was deafening and it felt a little chaotic. Laughter and a buzz of excitement filled the air and more and more people filled the waiting area outside of the conference room.

Selfie after selfie was being taken as well as group pictures, no doubt to be uploaded to social media. I made my way upstairs to see if I could find Sarah and as luck would have it, she happened to be making her way down towards the basement. She greeted me with a big hug and told me how amazing the weekend was going to be. We made our way back downstairs and she introduced me to Katie, one of her TrueVisage friends. Katie looked familiar and Sarah reminded me that she had been at my first meeting in St Albans back in December. Katie was really pretty, tall and could easily have been a model. Although her general demeanour towards me was friendly, once again as with many of the other girls I was meeting, I couldn't help but shake off the feeling that it was all an act and just a little bit false. I doubt Katie would normally have given me the time of day, had it not been for the fact that Sarah had introduced me to her as her cousin. I guess looking back, all of us were in competition with each other. Yes, we had our own businesses, however we were selling the one thing, TrueVisage products – we were all competing for product sales and sign-ups.

After what seemed like hours, we were eventually herded into forming a queue and after the relatively quick checking off of names and ensuring we had all pre-paid our £50 ticket fee, we were all made to wait by the three large doors ready for them to be opened so we could get a seat. There was no seat allocation, it was basically a free for all, and it reminded me of the way you boarded a low-cost flight, and the way people run for the plane in order to bag the best seat. The doors finally opened and Sarah whispered in my ear that apparently Katie had already saved us some great seats close to the front – "just look out for Katie" she said. As the throng pushed forward, I scanned the room and as Katie was statuesquely tall, I located her quickly and we made our way towards what looked like the perfect place close to the stage. The room was filling up quickly and as we went to sit, Katie announced that she had reserved seating for her guests and that there were only two spare seats left in her row. There were four of us and as we didn't want to split up, Sarah said we would look elsewhere, it wasn't an issue – although Katie didn't seem too bothered that we wouldn't be sitting together.

By the time we had turned around the whole of the room was pretty much full, we luckily managed to find seats right at the back, two rows from the back in fact. It wasn't great, but at least we had seats.

There must have been about 600 to 800 people in the room. Once the room settled, all of a sudden, the lights went out, music started blaring and dramatic nightclub type lighting danced around the room to the beat of the music. Everyone began to cheer and clap.

This was the start of my TrueVisage journey and the beginning also of what I can only describe looking back now, as brainwashing and my introduction to the toxic positivity culture.

Chapter 10

I had never attended or heard of an event like this. It seemed innocent; however, these events are cleverly structured and worded to make attendees fall for the hype. When I look back now, I can see all the signs however at the time I, like many others who attended, fell for the spiel. The TrueVisage speakers begin with praising everyone for attending, as this is the first step to a brand new you and a brand-new career. You are continuously praised for your strength, courage and confidence. You are bombarded with love, the psychological term used is Love Bombing. TrueVisage will love you and help you to become a success. The speakers praise you for the fact that you have chosen to be the master of your own destiny and that you are taking the steps into becoming your own boss. You will no longer work for someone else, making someone else rich and their dreams come true whilst your dreams dwindle into nothing. Again, looking back, I would have said that we were all there making TrueVisage money but again, everything was worded and presented as though you were the main earner.

Two large screens were set up either side of the stage and photos of the TrueVisage Founders were displayed. The key speaker spoke about them as if they were Gods, because of them, we were being given a chance to be reborn and to begin a new life. It was almost like I was at a religious meeting. The Founders being compared to the likes of Jesus. We were told that becoming a part of TrueVisage was going to seriously alter our lives, however the only way this was going to happen, is if we truly embraced it. The speaker then went on to mention that the room was fully attended today, however as the weekend went on, only the true believers and the people who one hundred percent wanted to change and become successful would be left. It felt like a challenge, almost like we were being dared to leave

– stay if you want to become a success and change your life, leave – if you want to be a loser in life. The decision is yours.

A lot of what Anna said at my first meeting at St Albans was repeated, how you shouldn't live your life "tired of being tired", how you should be "living your best Life". They had a "scientist" come up onto the stage, who supposedly worked in the product lab and explained to us how the products were made and what made them so special. Everything was "Amazing" – this word gets used a lot amongst the people who are involved with TrueVisage. In fact, it's one word now that when I hear it, I think of TrueVisage. Never has a word been so overused.

Eventually, the event progressed onto the award ceremony, where the top earners were presented with their new pin titles, a small minority were given Blue Gems – basically a necklace with the TrueVisage Logo and a tiny blue stone set into it. Not the sort of jewellery I would personally wear, but I guess it means something to whoever wins it. To this day I still do not understand the meaning of all the many, many pin titles and badges, however I now realise that this is designed to keep you with TrueVisage for years and years, as it takes the vast majority of people years and years to acquire just the first few titles.

The majority of people with TrueVisage never win any pin tiles and never earn any real money. Of course, this was absolutely never mentioned at the Success Summit. It was also never mentioned between the people that represented TrueVisage. What was mentioned however was that if you failed, you did so because *you* don't trust in the process, *you* are attracting failure by thinking you will fail. There were various spokespeople who got up on stage to promote the power of Positive Thinking. One man was invited up onto the stage and did a trick with an arrow to promote the message of trust. This was all geared towards us trusting in the process, trusting in TrueVisage, trusting in the power of positive thinking. The concept of positive thinking and shunning all those around you who think negatively was forced down our throats the entire weekend.

As the award ceremony continued and whenever someone came up onto the stage, they would tell us their story about how miserable they were until TrueVisage discovered them. Remember, you don't find TrueVisage, TrueVisage finds you! All of the tales were rags to riches stories. One woman told us about how she was on benefits, a single mum. She was absolutely broke and couldn't afford to buy food for her child. She was then introduced to TrueVisage online (through Instagram) and with the little money she had, was encouraged by her Upline to borrow from her mum ("the best loan ever" were her words) she purchased the product Starter Pack (which I believe back then was £400) and began to promote the products on Facebook. Within weeks she had orders coming in and after just one year in the business, could afford a deposit on her own home. You could hear the sniffles from the crowd, people crying at all of the various testimonials of how so many people went from being broken messes to huge successes. Some of the stories were so farfetched, yet here we were believing them. Why would all of these people be here – everyone on the stage was so nice, so friendly, so full of love and positivity that it would be impossible for us to think they were lying to us.

Every now and then Sarah would turn to me and smile and tell me how amazing it all was. I felt like I had been specially selected to be here, like this was a private, exclusive club and I was being offered this gift of success and it wasn't costing me anything. We were told by the various speakers, that TrueVisage had taken care of everything for us in order to make running our businesses as simply as possible. We would have no overheads, no worries about product production, we wouldn't need to worry about accounts or human resources. All we needed to do was sell and recruit. It was that simple.

I personally think the power of positive thinking is a good thing. I am lucky in the respect that I have always been someone who looks on the bright side of life and tries to see the good in all situations, however looking back now, the way the message of positive thinking was delivered over the course of the Success Summit weekend was a little excessive, even for me. In fact, now I realise it was utterly toxic.

One of the speakers who was really hyped up over the weekend was an American, a self-made millionaire who was also supposedly working as a TrueVisage representative. From the very beginning I thought this was farfetched and he absolutely did not strike me as someone who worked in this business. I believe to this day that he is just a paid motivational speaker. He bounded up onto the stage full of life, whooping and high fiving people in the audience. He told his story of how for years and years a friend had tried to convince him to join TrueVisage and he had always refused. He spoke of how he was a business man, who had made and lost, then made and lost his fortune again and again.

Until one day his friend contacted him again and invited him to a Success Summit, just like this one. He was overcome with emotion and began to cry as he told us how his life had changed and once he adopted all of the amazing advice from his friend (his Upline), and watched the online tutorial and attended every single meeting and event religiously, his life changed. He told us about his father, who was his mentor and that he once said to him "Son, show me your friends, and I'll show you your future". The conference room went silent. He looked around the room and said that if we wanted to be a success, we needed to ditch all of the people around us who were unsuccessful in life, time wasters and no hopers, as this was what we would attract. We needed to surround ourselves with like-minded people, people who are driven and focused on succeeding, as this was ultimately what we would become.

Before the American Motivational Speaker left the stage, he promised he would be back for the second part of the summit tomorrow, with more on how to make our businesses a success. He left the stage to a huge round of applause, whooping and high fiving all the way to his seat at the very front of the stage. There were three tables reserved at the front for all the "top earners" or what I know realise was the area where all of the paid TrueVisage Motivational Speakers and Brainwashers sat.

Chapter 11

Eventually, after a head spinning and intense morning, we broke for a late lunch. My head was fit to burst and I remembered I had the rest of the day and Sunday still to go. Sarah had disappeared and I was on my own again and as I was making my way back from having picked up a quick sandwich and coffee for the hotel café upstairs, I recognised a woman who had been sitting close to us in the row in front and as she smiled back at me I made my way over to her. As we got chatting, we both agreed how energetic the first part of the day had been and we swapped stories about how we were introduced to the business. She was a mum of one, who was sick of her job, wanted to work from home so she could be with her little one. She was super nice and we hit it off and spent the rest of the day sat together, as whoever was sitting next to me didn't turn up for the rest of the day. No doubt, they knew it was all a scam and made a quick getaway. I wish they had taken me with them; then again, would I have listened?

The second part of Saturday began and the next speaker was a man, who quite frankly, even at the time I thought was an absolute bully. I took an immediate dislike to him, despite the fact that Sarah tried to convince me that his behaviour was "just his way" and that he was so "funny". One of the other women, who was in our group explained that he was simply applying "tough love" and spoke this way in order to motivate us. I didn't think he was funny at all and unfortunately, unbeknown to me at the time our paths would cross again in the future.

Mike (or Mr Bully as I nicknamed him) was aggressive throughout his talk, however he tried to cover it up with the fact that he described it as "his passion shining through". He got up on stage and immediately started calling people out about their body language. Some poor man in the second row who had his arms crossed became his first target, "Hey you! Don't you want to be here?

What's your problem?" the poor man's face appeared on the big screen and he looked perplexed and a little horrified. He uncrossed his arms and Mike told him that was better. Mike explained that crossed arms signified aggression and disinterest, which was rich coming from him, especially the aggression bit.

He then reiterated the message about negative forces in your life and that anyone against you in your business venture is just jealous and wants to see you fail. This applied to family and friends. He told us that his "Circle got small, but his vision got bigger". I remembered the same quote from Anna at the St Albans meeting. He said that the main obstacles you would come up against in your quest for success would be family and friends. They would put your business down and try to convince you to give it up. They would be known as "Dream Stealers". He also drilled into us that we shouldn't be victims; we should be bosses.

According to the message TrueVisage put out, anyone you know or don't know who is negative towards you or the TrueVisage business you should cut out of your life. Period. Family are by no means excluded from the culling. One man who got up on stage as Mike's guest explained how when he first started the business, when he tried to recruit friends, they laughed him off and told him there were not interested in joining up. They also refused to buy any of the products. Mike's guest explained "I could see that they were jealous of me becoming a success and felt threatened by this, I didn't think it was wise to associate myself with them anymore". He said that in his mind the message was clear "Your Vibe attracts your Tribe".

Mike then went on to deliver his final key message. Surround yourself with like-minded people, people who want to see you succeed. People who are like you, positive and who want to take this business seriously. TrueVisage will become your new family if your current one lets you down. At the time, I agreed – I couldn't see the underlying danger to what was being pumped into my brain.

I watched video clip after video clip of people all over the world, particularly in America who had changed their lives by following the principles set out by TrueVisage. Photos of the TrueVisage founders displayed again on the huge screens like Gods for us to worship – the whole room erupting in applause and whoops rising up from everyone. People where high fiving all around me, hugs and smiles filled the room, everyone was whipped up in the positive vibes that filled the room, hungry to change their lives and become a success peddling beauty product and signing people up in the process.

They made it sound so easy, who wouldn't want to buy these amazing products, after all, people need them, who doesn't wash their hair, brush their teeth, take supplement, wear makeup – everyone does, surely everyone I know will rather buy from me than their local high street shop? It's a win-win situation.

The rest of the Summit format for Saturday was more testimonials and speeches from the people who had already been up on stage. They simply elaborated more and explained how they had become successful. These were people like me who had taken a risk and had put their faith in positive thinking, the law of attraction and TrueVisage. There were tears and laughter as real life success stories were paraded in front of us, one after the other. One of the faces of TrueVisage, the ultimate success story was by a woman called Emily. She came up onto the stage and told us her story. She started her business with just 24 followers on social media which has now grown into thousands (I think she has 7,000 on Instagram – at the time, she had 24,000 – it seems like nothing when you think of the numbers some people have, but compares to my 300 followers, it was a huge amount to me). She earned every pin title imaginable and all of the huge commission pins. The ultimate award being the one-million-pound commission pin, which means she has made a million pounds in commission from TrueVisage.

Her message was clear, if she could do it, you could do it. If YOU really believe in yourself, if YOU work hard, if YOU focus on your goals to becoming the successful Director of your own company, if YOU cut out negativity from your life (and yes, we were also shown a video of one woman who actually divorced her husband due to the fact that he wouldn't support her TrueVisage dream), you too, could be standing on this stage picking up your pin title necklace – still to this day I have no idea why I thought that was the be all and end all or what it actually means to have one of those necklaces.

I actually think looking back that a lot of the so-called top earners, are probably being paid by TrueVisage to represent them and make out that they had succeeded. These people are used as tools to sell the dream. They attend all of the summits and big events and tell you the same stories over and over again, word for word. It all seems a little too staged for my liking, however this is just my opinion, maybe they are the small percentage and I do mean a very small percentage of people who succeed, however they do so on the shoulders of hundreds and hundreds who fail. When a director of a business employs you to work for them, yes, they do become successful and wealthy, however they also pay you money regularly to help them grow their business. With TrueVisage, the vast majority become poor, whilst someone above you is being sent on a reward holiday – yet no one questions this.

The difference with a Multi-Level-Marketing is that you are not paid a monthly salary, you get paid only if you sell stock or recruit. If you don't do this, you get nothing, whereas the person at the very top of the pyramid will earn money. That's the difference. They will earn by convincing you to buy stock and you need to do the same to the people below you. The lower down you are, the harder it becomes. That's why so many people fail. Not because of the law of attraction, not because they didn't keep their positive thinking up. It's because these schemes only benefit the small percentage of people right at the very top of the pyramid. Earning a pin title isn't a permanent thing, you have to keep up your level of sales in order to keep your pin title and progress to the next one. The only way to do this is to keep up your level of sales. You will be told to do this by your Upline by purchasing more products. Whether you sell them or not is your concern, your Upline has already profited and those above your Upline. In the early days of me being with TrueVisage I wasn't made aware of this.

After day one of brainwashing was over, I went back to mum and dads and told them about the event and what it was I was planning to do. My mum, being the wonderful typical mother that everyone should be blessed to have, was excited for me and said that as long as I was happy, she too was happy and that obviously, if Sarah had introduced me, it had to be legit and good no? Being a typical Italian mother, she too trusted Sarah wasn't leading me up the garden path so to speak. My dad on the other hand, although supportive, is way more mistrusting of people, including family and warned me that it could be a Pyramid scheme and that I should be careful.

Brainwashed for the day and still riding high on the good (toxic) vibes of the event, I immediately reassured him that it wasn't a scheme, the company was solid and that I would be my own boss. The potential to earn thousands a reality. Not wanting to crush my enthusiasm, my dad agreed and made one last point at telling me to be careful but left it there. Off to bed I went, my head full of TrueVisage dreams of one day owning the stage and telling my own success story to everyone attending.

Chapter 12

Sunday morning arrived and I bound out of bed and into another taxi to whisk me off to the training day section of Success Summit, during which Sarah reassured me I would learn loads of "amazing" things to help me start my business.

This time, we had managed to secure a round table (the seating format was different on day two, no longer rows of seats, instead round tables of 8, as there were less people in attendance).

At the start of the Sunday training, the woman on stage congratulated us on being the sensible ones attending today, which meant we were serious about growing our businesses. We were welcomed to the TrueVisage family as being like-minded people, who wanted to change our lives. The tips provided were from the top earners in the business, the same faces from Saturday showing us how we could gain more followers on social media, how to properly promote ourselves online as well as how we should behave going forward in our day to day lives.

As we now represented TrueVisage, we were not allowed to post certain things on our social media and there were rules, which considering we were supposed to be our own business owners seemed a little strange. On our Instagram and Facebook, we were not supposed to post any political views, or religious views. No photos of drunken nights out or revealing clothing. We had to remember we were TrueVisage brand ambassadors, everything we posted needed to be done in order to attract others to want to sign up. No vulgarity or brashness, no naked pictures. You were representing the products, therefore pictures posted needed to be of you ideally made up using TrueVisage products only. When we posted a product, we were advised to cover up the name and logo, as this would cause "intrigue" amongst your followers and tended to lead to people wanting to know more about it – you were effectively reeling people in. It's funny, not once did I think "hang on, Sarah did this to me…."

We were told we needed to throw away everything in our bathroom cabinets which could be replaced with TrueVisage products immediately, after all, if you want people to buy the products, they need to see you using them. In my mind I could imagine how much commission Sarah would earn on my purchases. I could see the whole way up through her Uplines, and their Uplines. I'll be honest and say that every time I did buy something, I couldn't help but think how much Sarah was getting. However, I couldn't be angry as she was family after all, and as explained at the Success Summit, wouldn't you rather put money in a friend or family members pocket, than a stranger? The whole of the Sunday training was basically geared to moulding us into TrueVisage Clones, constantly reiterating the positive thinking message, the success message, how we were now one big family.

We were told to "stand on the shoulders of giants" meaning, to look at what all the successful women and men who were working the business were doing and copy them, as this was a sure-fire way to becoming a success yourself. If I had any doubts about following this path before that weekend, they were brainwashed out of me. Before the end, Mike (Mr Bully) came back onto the stage with the American Motivational Speaker and reminded us all about the super exciting European Success Summit that was happening in May in Spain. We were told that if we were truly serious about becoming a success, we absolutely needed to attend. This was a business trip, an investment. The two huge screens lit up and began playing the promo video of the trip, which used footage from last year's European Success Summit. This cleverly put together video showed all the usual top earners, parading about in Summer kaftans, looking glamorous and telling us all that the European Summit was a fixed date in their calendars.

Anyone who is anyone in TrueVisage attends and it's basically one big party, where you also learn how to become a huge success. If you want to grow your business, earn more money than you have ever dreamed of and want to change your life, book your ticket now! The video ended and Mike began pointing at random people in the audience and asked them if they had booked their ticket. Most people hollered out "yes!", however he then pointed at a painfully shy woman who made the fatal mistake of saying "no". Mike asked her "why?" The woman explained that she had two small children and couldn't leave them at home with anyone.

Mike fished out his car keys from his pocket, a Mercedes by the look of the keyring. He then asked the woman "If I put these keys on that high wall over there, and promised you that you could have my car if you got the keys, would you find a way to get them?"

"Yeah!" was her reply to which we all laughed.

"Then why can't you find a way to attend the Summit, a trip that will change your life and guarantee you can buy your own Mercedes?" came his reply.

The room was deathly quiet. She responded that she couldn't afford the ticket, being a single mum. Mike's reply was that she should borrow the money, as had the other single mum on benefits in order to buy the Beauty Starter Kit.

Mike bellowed at her that she was just looking for excuses. He told her to ask her mum for the money and to look after the kids. At the end of the day, if she really wanted it, she would find a way.

This was the message to all of us. It was of the upmost importance that we attended all meetings and events. No excuses! Mike then handed over to the American Motivational Speaker who repeated his rags to riches story and what his dad had told him, just in case we had forgotten from yesterday. He then motivated us more by showing us photos of his massive house in the States, his huge swimming pool and Louis Vuitton luggage, his fast cars and pictures of him travelling business class on flights. He told us that if we wanted this life, we had to work hard and be part of TrueVisage, just like him. Finally, he ended with playing what he described as the perfect song to end the weekend "This is me" from The Greatest

Showman – another cringe moment, but I was whipped up in all of the "Love Bombing" I had experienced over the weekend and I wanted to be part of the TrueVisage family.

Over the course of the weekend, I had gained followers on Instagram, women who I had met at the Success Summit and who now also felt like friends. I felt part of a group of like-minded people, all wanted to change our lives and become successful. I felt good, I felt positive and for once in a long time, I felt I was working towards a greater goal. I had a purpose and was ready to succeed!

Chapter 13

I said goodbye to Sarah at the Summit as she was making her way home with some of the others by car and I knew it would be quicker by train. I left the hotel and made my way home with a head absolutely fit to burst with all things TrueVisage. I remember on my train journey home that I actually had a really bad headache and the bright lights of the carriage hurt my eyes. I still didn't think I would fit into this world of false lashes and nails; however, I was reassured by Sarah that not everyone was like that. I also realised that I could work my own angle and not be so similar to the other girls.

After all, I was thirty-nine and perhaps could appeal to the slightly older clientele. On my train journey home, I knew I had little choice but to make it work. I had left my job and made a commitment to this, I was going to make a success of it – I knew I could do it with the power of positive thinking and the law of attraction, just like we had been told over the weekend. Sarah messaged me just before I arrived home telling me she would call tomorrow, as she wanted to arrange a time to pop round so that she could explain the pay structure more and set me up on the tutorial videos.

James and I had of course kept in touch over the weekend, and when I arrived home, although keen to answer his questions about the event, I was mentally exhausted, my head was pounding and despite the pain behind my eyes, I wanted to see what people had posted on their Instagram about the summit. I had been posted avidly over the weekend and had noticed that lots of people had viewed my short videos on Instagram. This too was the start of my constant use of social media, which felt like at addiction.

Before TrueVisage, I very rarely used Social Media, back when Facebook was first launched, I was one of the late users, setting up an account page way after most of my friends and family had. I used

Facebook for a couple of years before deciding one day, whilst on holiday that I was in actual fact, sick of seeing people's lives on display, all of the advertisements and silly videos constantly clogging up my page, it just didn't appeal to me anyone. I decided then and there to delete my account. I immediately felt better for it, James followed suit and deleted his also. We felt liberated.

Years passed, then one day my sister Dani introduced me to Instagram. Initially I was disinterested, I thought it was just another Facebook, however she explained that it was much better, just photos and videos and much more creative and pleasant to use, less of people "washing their dirty laundry in public". I had a look and thought it looked fun. I set up a profile and slowly started to post pictures. Again, the addiction quickly took hold and I was constantly checking it. It was too much and decided to make a point of taking week long breaks from Instagram, where I would discipline myself not to check my phone as much.

Then TrueVisage came along. The whole Network Marketing business relies heavily on the use of social media, and before I knew it, I was mindlessly checking my phone, and it became a problem. When Sarah and I arranged a meeting at my place a couple of days after the Summit, she explained that in order to build my beauty business I would have to become more active online in order to build up my followers. When I began my "business" I had very few followers on Instagram, in truth it never really bothered me. It was never my intention to earn money from Instagram or to become an Influencer. I had about 300 followers on Instagram, however I did notice that the big TrueVisage earners had thousands and this did concern me.

Sarah reassured me that the followers would increase, I simply had to become more active, posting every day; posting about my lifestyle and the products. I remember laughing about this and telling Sarah that my life wasn't really that interesting! This is when she mentioned that it was all about "Attraction Marketing". I remember the TrueVisage Speakers at the Summit had explained this also.

I had to actively seek out things to post about and make the most mundane of activities look interesting. Sarah told me to look at what the other girls were posting and basically do the same, remember: "Stand on the shoulders of Giants".

She also insisted that I would need to open up a Facebook account. I was deflated upon hearing this, as I really wanted to avoid Facebook, however Sarah explained that all of the online tutorials were on the TrueVisage Facebook page and one of our major Uplines regularly posted live tutorials (which I now translate as more Brainwashing) in order to keep the "Success message" fresh in our minds. It wasn't compulsory that we watched the videos, however it was strongly recommended that we did so in order to succeed and of course, we wanted to do well and earn lots of money, so I swallowed my pride and set up my new LindaBeauty Facebook account.

Sarah also added me to two new TrueVisage WhatsApp Groups, explaining that one group was for all new comers to TrueVisage, where we were welcomed to the business and we could use this group to obtain any information about the products and future meetings and Zoom tutorials. The other group was larger and in all honestly was pretty much the same as the other group. I admit, I was a little perplexed as to why we had two separate groups, however I went along with it as I guess at first it felt nice be included and be part of the True Visage family.

I admit at the beginning, I did feel a little overwhelmed with using Facebook again, as it had changed quite a bit since I had last used it, and I felt it was less user friendly. I found the constant pinging of my phone from Messenger was a little annoying also, it was as if I needed to read all the messages coming through and be part of when was being discussed. The majority of the time, the messages didn't relate to me and most of the times, two or three of the girls would just have mindless conversations amongst themselves using the group. It got to point where I would mute the group or simply silence my phone so that I could have a break from it all. The constant pinging of messages all through the day and into the evening was one of the things I hated the most. It felt like a chain around my neck and turned me into a slave to my phone.

Chapter 14

One of the fundamental things which was covered at the Success Summit and which Sarah reminded me of was The List. I had to create a list of everyone I knew and I mean *everyone*. I had to begin with family, so mum, dad, my brother and sisters, then my siblings' partners. Aunts, uncles, cousins, their partners and any children, as long as they were eighteen years or over. I then moved onto my friends, their partners (even if I didn't know them very well). I had to include colleagues (ex-colleagues now), their partners, people who I knew in my community like the ladies who worked in my local drycleaners, the postman, any couriers, ladies who worked in my local coffee shop. I literally had to create a list of people and extend the web to everyone linked to them. This would be the beginning of my potential customer base.

When I looked at the list, I felt relatively comfortable contacting my family and friends, however there were quite a few people on the list that I was a little embarrassed about contacting, people who I hadn't spoken to in years. When I expressed my feeling of unease to Sarah, she asked me if I wanted to succeed in the business? Did I want to make money and begin to build a following? Of course, my response to this was yes – the answer therefore was simple.

I need to swallow my pride. I needed to stop being selfish and begin making sacrifices. This meant contacting everybody on my list and subtly mentioning my business and asking people if they were interested. I couldn't bulldoze my way into this, there was an art to it.

Before beginning what, I can only describe now as the most cringeworthy time of my life, I thought it would be wise to watch a few Facebook tutorials to see how the "Giants" of TrueVisage were doing it. I fired up my laptop and began trawling through video after video which pumped the message of success into my brain, covering what had been mentioned at the Success Summit and more. The video explained that this business was a "people" business, if you were shy or lacked confidence in speaking to people, you needed to work on improving this first.

We were advised to perhaps ask our Upline to help when we called people. By hosting a three-way call so that our Upline was present and would help us to navigate any questions your potential customer or downline may have. This was also a sure way to boost your confidence and teach you how to tackle any future calls. The process that was taught to us was a process which was explained to me the first time at my meeting in St Albans, then again at the Success Summit. It is also how Sarah introduced me to TrueVisage and how I went onto be ensnared by TrueVisage.

It went something like this, however there are small tweaks which can be made so that you can implement this to Instagram, Facebook or direct by phone:

Make initial contact with someone from your list. This can be done in person, or by social media.

Begin by making small talk, ask them how they are, ask how their family is etc.

Establish if there is something going on in their life which is causing them to complain, i.e. their job, low income, lack of time for themselves (Their "pain or weakness").

Let your potential Downline or customer know what you're doing, explain that life is great, that you have been introduced to this amazing way of earning an extra income which means you have more money, time, freedom to work from home. The person you have called will no doubt ask you what this is.

At this stage, you tell them nothing. You explain that you have a video link you can send them and that there is a meeting coming up soon. Your TrueVisage group will host monthly meetings. These meetings are exactly like the one I went to in St Albans and are designed for Uplines to bring potential signups to in order to introduce them to the business, just like Sarah did with me. I was still at this stage completely blinded by the fact that this is exactly what Sarah had done with me.

The video link which you send doesn't give much away, however provides enough information to intrigue people into wanting to know more.

If the person is interested, you send them the link and explain that you will follow up again in a day or two. Never leave your follow up any longer than this. The whole point to put pressure on the person and fix a date for your next call. If all goes to plan, you will finish the conversation with a time and date fixed for your call.

You then let your Upline know when the proposed call is set for, in case they feel that it should be a three-way call.

If, however they show signs of not being interested, you ask them if they know of anyone who would perhaps be interested in a way of earning at extra income and of wanting to improve their lives.

Again, if they say they will let you know, you fix a date and time for a follow up call on this. You never end the call with simply letting them go, either way you will have a follow up date and time fixed. We were taught to overcome obstacles and not to take no for an answer.

This method is blatant harassment and I cringe at the technique used. It's also a blatant sales call and thankfully, I never employed most of the above. I tried to make my calls and contact as natural as possible, however I was being contacted everyday by Sarah, wanting to know "how I was getting on with the list" as I am sure, she was being pressured by her Upline, Chloe. I simply couldn't force my friends, family and acquaintances into doing something they didn't want to do and I refused to damage relationships. Maybe this is why when I walked away from it all, I thankfully, still had all my relationships intact and perhaps this is why I didn't find it hard to break away. Others I know are less fortunate and I believe this is why so many people feel that they can't stop. That if they do, they have damaged so many relationships, that they have nothing to go back to so they are stuck. This is precisely where TrueVisage wants you.

After watching the TrueVisage "Greats", I finally plucked up the courage and began making contact with people. I had received my new beautiful business cards; I was a Director (eye roll) of my own beauty business and I celebrated by bragging on Instagram. My first post for LindaBeauty was of my business card and some text beside the photo, explaining that going forward I was my own boss, a Director! I had officially set up a beauty business. I received lots of congratulations from friends and family and I felt super proud of myself. Proud of what, I'm not sure. When I look back, I realised of course that it was all a lie. I wasn't responsible for the branding and packaging of the products. I didn't keep any stock or hire anyone. I didn't own the TrueVisage brand name, I didn't decide on the prices, therefore why did I believe I was a business owner? Most of my posts on social media were of me bragging about how great my life was. I worked for myself, had time to leisure about in the garden, in doors, on at my local coffee shop, working my business from my phone which basically translated into posting bragging photos on Instagram in order to entice people into joining up to TrueVisage.

I had basically achieved nothing. I had a catalogue of beauty products which were not my own. All I was doing was selling someone else's products and encouraging people to sign up under me so that they could do the same. I was hardly Sir Alan Sugar – I was just a sales person working from home. In the mornings, I would get up and post about me washing my face with my Facial Cleansing Device and cleanser. It would take me ages to strategically place my phone in my bathroom, so that it captured me at the right angles. Posting pictures of products, carefully covering up the TrueVisage logo and name. I wouldn't outwardly ask people to buy, I would simply say how "amazing" my skin looked now that I was using this new "amazing, life changing" product.

My immediate family knew what I was doing, however funnily enough not one of them was beating down my door to buy my products or sign up under me to open an account.

I was determined not to pressure people; I didn't want to be a pushy sales person. I wasn't a ruthless business person and I naively and rather proudly believed that the products would sell themselves. I didn't have to beg people to buy TrueVisage, TrueVisage was that good, the products would simply sell themselves.

I wanted to believe in the products and business model so badly that the business didn't need to be pushed. It would happen naturally.

I worked my way down my contact list, everyone I contacted whether by phone, text, email, Facebook or Instagram told me that they weren't interested and that neither were the people they knew. I was shut down quickly by people, telling me it sounded like a Pyramid Scheme and that I should be careful. I was so brainwashed, that I became defensive and responded by defending my TrueVisage business, saying that it was no less a pyramid scheme than what you find in the average workplace – a Chief Executive at the top, with Directors below them, then managers, then supervisors, then the standard workforce, it was the same principle. This is what we were told by TrueVisage and this is what I believed. I wasn't going to let jealous people steal my dream.

One of the people on my list was my very first employer who owns a clothing business and who I still see from time to time when I pass his shop on the way to my parent's place in London. I called under the guise that I was after some "business advice". When I explained what I was doing, he too like many others warned me against the business. I was aware that he knew someone who owned a pharmacy and asked if they would be interested in stocking the products in their chemist. He doubted they would as the mark up on the products wouldn't be worth it. He explained to me that this was why the products were never stocked in shops. I ended the call thanking him however, I felt angry as it felt like he was belittling what I was doing and I felt insulted; however, in truth my main feeling was that of embarrassment and shame. I still to this day haven't walked past his shop to say hello as I normally do, which saddens me. This is one of the emotional and psychological scars I bear from being part of TrueVisage and I believe that being part of a MLM company really does ruin relationships. We used to be super close, he was a family friend and just like that, a 10 minute phone call and it's all gone.

Chapter 15

As the days rolled by, on I went working my way down the list, until it got to a point where I could no longer face the rejection and embarrassment. I even contacted an ex-boyfriend who politely declined and even warned me about TrueVisage, as his sister-in-law had been a representative years ago and had made very little after dedicating a year to it. I still wasn't prepared to listen; I was so blinded by the pure will to be a success and to think positive thoughts. I was so brainwashed by it all and I guess I craved the need to be part of this family who exuded positive vibes and love. No one could convince me that this was bad.

I had managed to get a little interest from my sister Dani and one of my cousins who popped round for a visit one weekend and I showed them the few products I had. I look back at that visit and realise just how desperate I sounded. Pushing products which were average at best, looked cheap, yet were extortionately priced. When I showed my cousin one of the lip glosses which cost £21, she pointed out that she tended to spend around £5 on a well know high street beauty brand. She asked if I had any she could look at, to which I responded no, and she asked how she would know which shade to buy without trying it first, something she could do on the high street. Committing to £21 before buying was a bit much and she was right, she wouldn't be able to return it. I would have to give her a refund and I would then be stuck with a lip gloss I would be unable to sell or use. The colour shades in the catalogue were not the best representation either.

I posed this question on one of the TrueVisage WhatsApp groups and the girls replied back that I had to tell people that the products were "Amazing!" They wouldn't regret buying them and that they were worth every penny. Sarah told me to really sell the products, by telling people I had used them and that they were brilliant. I didn't like the idea of lying, I mean, I was happy to promote products on Instagram that had I used and genuinely liked, but to say that a product was good when I had not had first-hand experience in using it wasn't how I wanted to run "my" business.

Sarah helpfully pointed me in the direction of the shared TrueVisage Facebook page which was loaded with "testimonials" on products each representative and their customers had used. The page was a catalogue of before and after pictures which we could use on our social media in order to promote the products. The whole process was something I wasn't really comfortable with, however all the other girls were doing it and bragging about how many orders they had flooding in, I guess I had no other option, as at this stage I wasn't making any money and needed to use whatever tools I had at my disposal.

The Facebook tutorial videos also mentioned reading books about Network Marketing and Positivity. According to all the successful TrueVisage Representatives, you needed to attract positivity and dispel all negative thoughts. It was your sole responsibility to "think" your business into being a success and if your business was failing, well, this was simply down to your negative mindset and the fact that you were attracting failure. I ordered most of the books recommended and immediately began to fill my mind with positive thoughts, the Law of Attraction and all things Network Marketing related. Some of what was written in the books was actually quite good and as mentioned before, I agree with keeping your thoughts positive as much as possible and applying a positive mindset to my life in general. However, now when I look back, this was forced and not the natural, healthy way to implement such thoughts.

The fact that my business failed was because I attracted failure - that I disagree with and I strongly believe this was purely a mind control tactic applied by TrueVisage to pass all blame onto you. I worked tirelessly to promote my "business" and the products. The fact of the matter is that MLM business are saturated. The products are cheap and overpriced. You can spin it in as many ways as you like, however what I was involved with was a pyramid scheme and they are set to fail for 99.9% of the people who sign up for them. A small percentage, those at the top will succeed, however during my time with TrueVisage my suspicions grew about the legitimacy of their success claims.

As my TrueVisage journey continued, along with brainwashing my mind with literature, I stopped reading books I was interested and pretty much replaced my entire library with Multi-Level-Marketing and Network Marketing books. I also began to evaluate my appearance. Once again, looking at what the girls were doing on Instagram and how Sarah presented herself, I took to having fortnightly manicures, making sure my eyebrows were neat and my hair was washed and blow dried everyday so that I would look good in any photos I posted onto my social media. I began to dress differently and took on the cloned appearance of all the other girls in a bid to boost my followers. I made sure that every day, I woke up early, went for a swim - most of the TrueVisage Clones practiced Yoga and, in a bid to keep a little of my identity I did something I really enjoyed. I would then come home and ready myself for the day.

Again, going back to when Sarah told me to upload anything about my life in a bid to attract followers and promote this amazing lifestyle, I would take my laptop and work journal to my local coffee shop and post pictures of me "working" from my local coffee shop captioned with "Being my own boss means I can work my business from anywhere". I wasn't giving too much away, simply dangling juicy morsels of my great life to people who I hoped would message me to find out more. The picture would be of my laptop and a cappuccino, no mention of the products or business directly.

No one messaged me. I would post pictures of me in loungewear, saying that my commute was simply downstairs and I didn't have to be suited and booted for work – nothing, no messages.

This continued for weeks and although my following increased to approximately four hundred (mostly TrueVisage representative doing the same thing as me), I still had no orders or people enquiring about signing up.

Chapter 16

The TrueVisage online tutorials also mentioned striking up conversations with people when you were out and about. After all, you had to grow your List of Contacts every day. This meant approaching strangers and "Fishing" online. I have always been quite confident in striking up conversations with people and was becoming quite good at subtly mentioning my business to people. I remember one morning whilst in my local coffee shop which was becoming my go to place during the week, a young girl in her late teens was having a conversation with her mum at the table next to mine. She was lamenting about how much she hated her supermarket job and didn't want to be stacking shelves for the rest of her life. Her mum was encouraging her to look for something else.

I felt like this was a sign from the universe, this could be my first sign up! I looked over and as when the girl eventually made eye contact with me, I smiled and admitted that I had overheard their conversation and that I too was in a similar situation only a couple of months ago. My life had now changed and it was all down to the business opportunity I would be more than happy to introduce her to. I could see that the mum felt a little bit uneasy, however she politely smiled back and asked me what I was doing. Of course, I couldn't give too much away – if I told her she would be peddling beauty products online and trying to get people to do the same, she would probably decline there and then. Instead, I gave her one of my business cards and told her to drop me an email. She asked if I owed my own Beauty Shop, to which I said no. I simply told her to email me and I would provide her with more information. They both got up and left, as they had finished their coffees, or perhaps they thought I was strange! I arrogantly thought that my mysterious introduction would leave this girl chomping at the bit. Needless to say, I didn't hear from her. Her mum no doubt warned her of the potential scam.

I felt dishearten as I would look at what all the other girls were doing, which was exactly like what I was doing, yet they were bragging on Instagram and Facebook about huge orders being placed and finding the time to respond to all of the messages in their inboxes.

As the days passed, I couldn't understand what I was doing wrong. When I looked online, at the Instagram and Facebook pages of the other girls, they were posting photos of boxes full of products which they bragged they would be soon distributing to their customers. Sarah was doing it too – boxes and boxes of toothpaste, shampoo and makeup. How were they managing to get all of these orders and I wasn't getting a peep out of anyone, not even family? Despite the fact that I was positively thinking myself into oblivion every day. The only deliveries I was posting about were my own, making out that these were for my "customers". It was embarrassing. Yet I felt like I couldn't lose face online. I was being watched by my followers and I didn't want to fail or show to be failing, especially friends and family. I felt like I had a point to prove after bragging about being a Director of my own Company.

I had connected with a good friend of mine who wanted to know more about what I was doing. This was also the beginning of my awful attitude to seeing every single friend or family meet up as a potential way to plug my business. I kid you not, I even shamelessly sold shampoo to my aunts' friend at a funeral, that's how bad and desperate this business made me. My friend and I met in London for lunch one day during the week, and I was armed with a copy of the TrueVisage product catalogue (which we had to pay for and they were quite pricey). After our initial catch up she then asked me why I had left my job and what had got me into this business.

She was, at the beginning of our conversation, really excited for me, however once she began to realise that it was a pyramid scheme, her face fell a little and she, just as many others had, warned me to be careful. I was determined not to let her negativity phase me and confidently told her that I knew what I was doing. I gave her the product brochure to flick through and she said that in actual fact she wanted to upgrade her beauty products and that she would look at the brochure and let me know if anything appealed to her.

I quickly mentioned that if she opened up an account, sighing up as my Downline, she would have access to her own wholesale account and that she would save 40% on the cost of the products, however she said she wanted to support me in my new business and was happy to buy at full price from me. When I look back now, being the true friend that she is, she only did what she did out of pure friendship to me. A few days later, she contacted me saying that she wanted to buy the facial cleansing device and cleanser to go with. I had the same device, which was over £200 and I was amazed! My very first sale! I made £40 from this sale in commission and although small, it felt like £4000. I was so pleased. Finally, all of my positive thinking and patience had paid off.

Sarah was so proud of me and when I announced my sale on the group WhatsApp everyone gushed at how amazing it was. Sarah reminded me to post the commission notification message from TrueVisage onto my Instagram – not the amount, just the fact that I had made money. I wasn't entirely happy about doing this and asked why I should brag and she said it was all about "Attraction Marketing". She explained that we sometimes have to over exaggerate stuff in order to attract people to the business. Sarah also mentioned the time when she went to exchange her car which she had on finance and was leased. I remember she had posted a picture of herself standing next to a really expensive car saying that she was so lucky that due to her successful business, she was able to upgrade her car. I was then surprised when she turned up at mine with the exact same standard model, she had been driving the day before.

I asked her about the super car and she said she had changed her mind. Thinking back, it had all been just a lie, posting false pictures to give the illusion of you living your best life, when in actual fact, you were just false advertising. This is how naïve I had been.

Chapter 17

I had made my first sale and this spurred me on. I went on to sell a couple of small items to just family and friends. It was a very small amount, an order here and there, the amount I was making was nothing in comparison to my outgoings. I was buying products for myself to use and promote and even though I was saving using my wholesale account and the account I had set up under James's name so that I could make a small commission from his orders. I know, it's ridiculous to think that ordering items through James's account would brining in a few pennies, but it all added up to in my commission account and towards my pin title. Every little bit helped – it also meant I had a sign up under my name, even though it was just my husband. Sarah explained she had done the same and had also signed up her mum and step-dad, as well as her Godmother.

Having a Facebook account did help a little, and I linked it to my Instagram so in actual fact I didn't really need to post much to it – it pretty much managed itself. The only product enquiries I was receiving were though Facebook. I used the pre-prepared before and after pictures from the TrueVisage databank and I would receive the odd message asking me about the products, however, as soon as I responded with a price, the enquiry went dead. I used the over exaggerated before and after pictures (which I knew deep down were fake) of the lip plumping balm, at £24 and received no intertest. A "natural" Botox Cream at nearly £60, no one I knew would pay such prices and no strangers were going to part with their cash either. I had these products and, in all honesty, there was absolutely nothing special about them. James hated the toothpaste and said it tasted funny and for all the amazing reviews about how white it made your teeth and all of the before and after pictures, which were totally edited and fake, my teeth never became whiter. I used three tubes continuously, and my teeth felt cleaner only after going back to the well-known brand I used to use.

I also convinced James to buy the mint face scrub and he laughed at the fact that it was basically the toothpaste with grains in it. He was right! The mint face scrub was exactly the same as the toothpaste, just that the texture was abrasive. He told me it was a con at over £20 and not to buy it again. James still supported me; however, he didn't like the products and expressed his views that he thought they looked cheap. I tried other angles and thought I would target businesses. I knew of a local all-women's gym in my area and I knew they stocked products, perhaps I could convince them to stock the TrueVisage range. I called and spoke to the gym administrator and as soon as I mentioned TrueVisage, she couldn't hang up quick enough.

I drew upon my knowledge from the positivity books I had read and would not be deterred. One of the books mentioned that you should try to make a game out of your cold calls and go for as many "no's" as you can, as eventually, a "yes" would come along.

I Googled the gyms name and discovered that they were a franchise, with about 60 gyms nationwide. I made a note of the areas and numbers and called them all. It was extremely time consuming and tiring to have to run through the same script on each call. Most just cut the call short and the women I spoke to said they weren't interested, some were polite and asked me to email, however I never heard from them despite my several follow up emails.

Only three showed an interest, with only one saying she was keen. Just one gym in Essex was interested and wanted to meet with me to look at some of the products and the Face Lift hand held device. This was the item I was going to promote the most. It was just under £300 retail and came with serums which needed to be used with the product at approximately £30 for a box of three treatments. I knew the gym had two treatment rooms and was excited at the prospect of selling this product to the owner. When I told Sarah, she was thrilled and said she would drive me there and be present at the meeting. I was pleased as I felt I needed someone with me with the experience to explain how the gadget worked.

The gym owner cancelled our meeting four times, before finally committing to a date, I truly thought she was going to cancel all together and felt a little messed around by her. However, I was desperate for her business, as apart from the one sale to my friend and a couple of small sales to my sister and mum, oh and the shampoo at the funeral, I had made no sales, therefore this was the break I needed. We agreed on a date in March and I looked forward to this being the beginning of my success.

It had only been two months into my business journey and I had spent quite a lot of money on products for myself. I needed the products in order to post pictures about using them on social media. I had also spent money on my business cards, which wasn't much, however I had absolutely no money coming in and was relying on my husband's salary and our joint savings. I knew I had rushed into it, and I guess I was hoping for too much. There was absolutely no way you could do this business whilst also working a full-time job. You had to dedicate hours to contacting people and posting online. The only way I could have committed 100% to this was to be at home. We were also told that dedicating yourself to the business full time would yield faster results. I was only two months into the business and knew that it was going to take time to build, however based on what everyone on social media and in our groups were saying and based on what Sarah was saying she earned, I was surprised I had yet to receive the flood of orders everyone bragged about in their early days.

I accepted that the majority of my business was going to come through orders and sign-ups from strangers. It would be a lot harder, but going by what the others were saying, it was doable.

I was also attended the regular meetings for our Hertfordshire group in St Albans and was made one of the senior people who helped to organise the meetings. This basically meant I contributed the £10 fee for the conference room hire and took payment on the evening from attendees. The format for the meetings was the same as the first one I attended back in December. TrueVisage Representatives hosting a scaled down version of a Success Summit, which looked very amateur and was put on for anyone bringing guests or potential sign-ups. It was an opportunity to explain what the business was about using the PowerPoint presentation and to hear successful testimonials. Most of the time, there would be only one or two guests, sometimes no one new would attend, yet we would run through the meeting without fail and again, this was just to refresh our minds, brainwash us more and ingrain the TrueVisage message into our brains.

During the course of the meetings, anyone who was still employed in a full-time job was made to feel like a failure. You were basically working to build someone else's dreams and earning money for the fat cats at the top.

At the time, I didn't think to question this, as wasn't it exactly what we were doing by working with TrueVisage – making money for the TrueVisage owners and people at the top? We were told that our ultimate goal was to be free of a boring, soul crushing jobs and to one day, be master of our own destiny and work for ourselves.

After only attending a few meetings, I decided that I actually didn't want to go to them again, and perhaps I would skip the odd meeting. The £10 fee was something I quite frankly couldn't afford as I had no money coming in, plus the petrol to get me to St Albans was just another unnecessary expense I could do without. When James asked me why I wasn't attending some of the meetings, I told him the truth and also said that it was extremely repetitive. Sarah was concerned when I skipped my first one. She too agreed about the repetitiveness, however said that it was a great opportunity to take photos to upload to social media. Again, it was a tool to use for Attraction Marketing, showing people that you were attending a business meeting in order to make your business a success. Meeting with likeminded, positive people who shared the same vision. Looking back, I guess the people who attended needed these meetings to validate what they were doing and to feel like they were important business people. I however saw them as a waste of time and money. I saw the same people, who talked about the same thing. I kept on attending as I didn't want to be thought of as someone who wasn't taking the business seriously. If my business failed, I knew this would be thrown at me as an excuse for my failure.

Chapter 18

Sarah messaged the WhatsApp group to tell us that there was another London event coming up. Sarah said she had all of the information and asked if I wanted to go. This meeting wasn't going to be as big as the January Success Summit, however there was quite a buzz about it, as the lady who was hosting was another top earner and had the coveted "one million commission earners" pin title. She was also Emily's Upline – another major face in the TrueVisage family who spoke at the January Success Summit. Sarah was keen for us to attend as we were bound to learn more about growing our businesses and becoming successful. As I still wasn't making any sales and had only managed to sign up my husband, I decided that I needed all the help I could get.

I packed myself off on a train to London one grey and bleak Saturday in February. Sarah had cancelled on me at the last minute and as I had already committed £40 for the ticket (Sarah reminded me this was an investment into my business) it looked like I would be attending on my own. The event was being held in Holborn, a part of London I knew well and the hotel was close to Russell Square Station and was actually quite nice. This was only a one-day event, which began at 10am and ended at 5pm, so at least I wouldn't have to stay the night.

I made my way inside and grabbed a quick coffee in the hotel bar. While I was queueing, I recognised the face of one of the girls who also regularly attending our St Albans meetings. It was nice to see a familiar face amongst all of the strangers. We got chatting and I asked how her business was doing. I was open and honest about my business, if someone asked me how I was getting on I would say that it was difficult, however I was new to the game and despite my frustrations, I couldn't really expect too much in the early days. I had made a few sales however wasn't getting anywhere with my family. I also added that I was keeping my vibes positive and was sure that one day soon, things would pick up.

I didn't get this from anyone else. It's weird when I look back as surely, even though we are all running our own business, ultimately, we are all doing the same thing, therefore I couldn't understand why nearly all of the women I spoke to were so cagey about their progress. It was almost like no one wanted to admit they weren't doing so well. I would be bombarded with how brilliantly things were and how much money they had coming in. Yet, deep down I could see by the look in their eyes that this wasn't true. I found out why so many people lied over the coming weeks.

Once inside the conference room, I grabbed a seat close to the front as this time around, I was determined not to be seated at the back. Despite the fact that my business wasn't making any money, I had grown in confidence due to all of the positivity books I had been reading and wanted to be seen as a participator. Kelly came up onto the stage, riling everyone with claps, whoops and cheers, all very American vibe. Just as in January, we were congratulated for being there and wanting to change our lives for the better.

Kelly was on stage with another women, Marie and together they brainwashed everyone in the room with exactly the same patter as was part of the January event. It was a mirror image of the previous months Success Summit. The business model was shown and explained, the same videos about how much better your life could be by being your own boss and getting back your life. Only two awards were handed out, these ladies had managed to sign up five people. There were testimonials, approximately ten women came up onto the stage to tell us how the business had changed their lives and made them better people. They were all still working their full-time jobs, however were running their TrueVisages gigs on the side and making extra money. It's funny, looking back, none of these women looked truly happy. Despite the smiles and enthusiasm, I couldn't help but think that they all looked tired, harassed and as if they were under a tremendous pressure.

I worked my business full time at home, and knew just how much I had to do and still wasn't making money. I knew full well that it was nigh on impossible to put the amount of work in as I was doing along with a full-time job, a commute to and from work, household chores and kids (and I didn't have any!) - you would be exhausted. I had heard of TrueVisage representatives encouraging women who were doing the above, to pop their kids into bed and begin plugging their businesses in the evenings, working way into the early hours. We were also encouraged to hire cleaners to take on household chores, so this would free up more of our time to dedicate to our businesses. If you had children, employ a nanny to look after them. Yes, this was an added expense, however we were told to view this as a business investment and in the long run, once we became successful – you would have way more time to spend with your family.

I couldn't see or understand it then, however I do now. We were being harassed and bullied by our Uplines to make sales and sign up as many Downlines as possible. Most of the women I spoke to were given targets and made to reach them, even if it meant spending their own money to make their goals. Luckily for me Sarah never did this and in truth, I would have refused. This was *my* business and I ran it how I wanted. The point of being "my own boss" was to not have to answer to Sarah. However, this was not the case for most of the women. Sarah was feeling the pressure from Chloe and I would soon begin to see the cracks.

I may have fallen for the scheme (although at the time I didn't see it); however, I was not a push over – one thing I am thankful for is that I refused to be bullied. As the Saturday meeting progressed, we were once again told to throw out all of our current non-TrueVisage products and replace the entire contents of our bathroom cabinet with TrueVisage skincare and beauty. In fact, in the training booklet I received from Sarah shortly after I signed up, we were told to replace approximately 25 products in our home with TrueVisage products. I did a rough calculation of what this would add up to, especially seeing at a deodorant alone cost £8, and the amount hit just over £560. If everyone did this, the Uplines stood to make a hell of a lot of money! We were also told once again to shun all negativity and negative people from our lives – which translates as anyone who cares about you and who warns you against entering a Pyramid Scheme you should cease all contact with.

Kelly and Marie were examples of true success, and we should use their examples and their experiences to aid us in reaching our goals. They both explained that they hardly used social media to build their business, they were "old school" and would pound the pavement, going into their local shops and business to pedal the products. We were told that we needed to go into our local hairdressers and nail bars with a bag full of products to sell and if no one wanted to buy, we should offer them the sign-up process. It wasn't just about the products Kelly explained, it was about the recruitment process as this is how you made your money.

My question was that if the person you approached didn't like the products or wasn't interested, why would they sign up? And once they signed up, how would you make money if they were not buying the products? I was sat next to two really nice girls, both in their early twenties and they were obviously new to the business. During our lunch break, we got chatting and they explained that they were here as Marie's guests. We friended each other on Instagram and Marie noticed we were talking from the other side of the room. One cardinal rule in Multi-Level Marketing or Network Marketing is that you never poach someone else's Downlines. This was obviously what Marie thought I was doing and stormed over to us, she sat down next to the girls and it was as if she were a lioness protecting her cubs. She asked the girls if they were enjoying the event and made a show of explaining the sign-up process to them. Her message to me was clear "back off, these two are mine". I had absolutely no intention of stealing her sign-ups away from her, it had honestly never occurred to me. This was how competitive this business is. TrueVisage spread the message of family and being nice and of positivity and kindness, however it is a dog eat dog world and everyone is out for themselves.

Before the afternoon was over, there was one last video that was to be shown. This video had also been played at the January Success Summit. It was about the second major Success Summit of the year, held in May in Spain. As explained in January, the event was going to be huge. Every year, TrueVisage held a Success Summit in May somewhere in Europe. Hundreds upon hundreds of people attending from all over the world. It was a two-day event, over a Saturday and Sunday with a big Dinner Dance on Sunday Evening.

It was the same beautifully put together marketing video played and was a montage of clips from the previous Success Summit which had been held in Marbella. We were assaulting with sun, sea, sand, cocktails and carefully selected TrueVisage Representatives telling us all how amazing the trip was. They had all learned so much from the trip, got to spend time with the best people who inspired them to achieve greatness. You would be crazy to miss it. "The time is now, what are you waiting for? Live you best life".

Kelly and Marie both stood in the middle of the stage and told us that if we were serious about growing our business, we absolutely had to attend this event. Just as the message had been drilled into us in January, once again we were being told that this was an investment into our business. The ticket for the event was £250 – I was still indecisive about going, it was a lot of money and although James and I had our savings, I felt awful dipping into it more than I already had. I also had to take into account that this excluded the price of the airfare and hotel, as well as spending money. Sarah has been harping on that she would need to buy new clothes, as everyone got glammed up and looked amazing out there, as you would be constantly uploading pictures onto your social media for attraction marketing. It was a huge expense and I wanted to go, but couldn't justify it.

Chapter 19

I arrived home and was in the middle of telling James how my day had gone when my phone pinged, it was a message from Sarah asking me how the event had gone. I was tired and hungry and just wanted to switch off, so I messaged her briefly saying it had been great. We arranged for her to come over on Monday, so we could work together. We had done this before and in truth, we never got any real "work" done. I guess it just made us feel important and it was yet another phoney post we could upload onto our social media about how busy we were working our businesses from home.

Sarah reminded me about the team Zoom call we had tomorrow at 8pm and that she would send over the details to join the meeting tomorrow. Apart from the constant pinging of my phone from the three WhatsApp groups I was now part of, and the messenger groups, and the regular St Albans meetings, we also had regularly weekly Zoom calls. Usually held on a Sunday or Monday evening, one of the higher graded Uplines would host, however we could all take turns and would pick a topic aimed to help us boost our sales. I thought the calls were pointless in truth, they didn't help and we just went over the same things every week. I felt the thirty-minute calls were for the Uplines benefit as they would use the calls to try to convince us to buy products, therefore boosting their commissions. I had no downlines on the call with me, I was simply on the call to boost attendee numbers. I always put on a brave face with James about TrueVisage and kept up my enthusiasm, he was always supportive, however I knew deep down he was simply waiting for me to stop and get myself a proper job.

It was time for the Zoom call the following evening. I would go upstairs into the bedroom so as not to disturb James. I logged onto the call using the ID and password Sarah had sent to me during the day. I logged in on time as always and patiently waiting for the other girls, approximately 10-15 in total to join the call. Once we were all online, the main speaker would welcome us and ask us how our week had been. A lot of us remained fairly quiet, as in truth we had nothing major to report, some of the girls would exclaim how they were great and doing well. The speaker would then turn to the topic in hand - boosting your online sales by posting lots of Attraction Marketing pictures (I was already doing this!). We should post of ourselves at home or in a café, telling people how we could work our business from anywhere. Post pictures of you with your children (if you had any) telling people how you could work your business whilst spending time with the kids.

We were told to brag about how much time freedom you had. Post pictures of you out shopping, telling people that this business allows you to buy stuff with all the spare cash you have. She said that we didn't have to actually buy anything, just try stuff on. This wasn't lying as such…it was more a case of "fake it till you make it". I loathed this slogan, and yes, it was lying. If I went into a shop and posted something on social media saying I was treating myself to a new bag, clothing or shoes, then I was. I wasn't going to lie about it. The call went on and on and it was always the same brainwashing drivel, keep up the positive thoughts, keep attracting positivity into your life and business and you will make sales and sign up lots of people. At this point nearly all of the positivity I felt was so forced and I suppressed so much of how I truly felt, I had no idea how much emotional and phycological damage this was actual doing to me. I think I experienced Imposter Syndrome way before it actually became a "thing".

I couldn't wait to ring off and was glad when the call was over. You could tell that the other girls didn't want to be on the calls, but it was part of the process and we had to show we were keen and that we wanted to participate. If one of the girls missed a call according to Sarah, it would be "noticed" as a sign that you weren't taking the business seriously. I remember Sarah telling me once that she had been at a Networking Marketing event one evening and a call was scheduled to take place at 8pm. She was driving back home from the event and actually pulled over in a car park in order to participate in the call. She knew her Upline, Chloe would be on the call too and was too afraid to miss it for fear of being reproached. Once again, I thought this was strange as we are supposed to be our own bosses, so why was she tolerating pressure from her Upline, who very much felt like her boss?

Sarah had mentioned she attended Network Marketing meetings in her area, and I was keen to do so also as I thought this would be a good way to meet new people and spread the word about my business. I did some research online and found several groups which were local and called the organisers to see if I could attend. All of the people I spoke to at first seemed friendly and keen for me to be part of their groups, however as soon as I mentioned that I was promoting TrueVisage their attitudes changed instantly. They told me that they didn't allow MLM company representatives to attend their meetings. I asked why and they explained it was because of the nature of the business and that in the past, many of the reps became quite bullish and forceful in their tactics to get people to sign up, that they decided it would be in the groups best interest to stop MLM company reps from attending.

It was really hard for me to hear this and it made me feel very much ashamed of what was doing. The Network Marketing organisers made me feel stupid and like I was representing a "dirty" company. They didn't take TrueVisage seriously at all. I quickly thought back to what was said at the Success Summit about people barriers and that these people were simple a negative influence. Dream Stealers - they simply didn't understand the business and I shouldn't waste my time with them. I kept on plugging away online and as luck would have it, I found a Network Marketing support group a stone's throw away from my home. It was held every Wednesday in a local hotel and as it was at 8am, breakfast was included during the meeting.

There was of course a cost to attend which was £12 and this included the cost of a full buffet breakfast which I thought wasn't too bad and I saw it as yet another business investment. I emailed the organiser and explained what I did and they were super friendly and happy for me to attend. They had another MLM company rep signed up, however this gentleman was representing another company which wasn't beauty or skincare so I was happy that I wouldn't clash with him.

I was super excited about being finally accepted into a Network Marketing group, I phoned Sarah with the good news. She was really pleased for me and advised me to bring a selection of products with me to show off, as well as the product catalogue. She also reminded me that it wasn't just about selling, I had to get sign-ups too, as this was where the big money was at and to upload plenty of posts on my social media about the fact that I was attending a "business meeting" – once again, all lies and all part of Attraction Marketing.

While patiently waiting for Wednesday's meeting, I kept ploughing my way through my Facebook contacts, looking at contacts of contacts and adding more and more people to my list. I had exhausted all of the people I knew and was now turning to what I would call the very last resort. People I really, really didn't want to contact; however, it was a last-ditch attempt to try to plug the products and get sign-ups. All of the tutoring videos on the TrueVisage Facebook page mentioned swallowing your pride and reaching out to everyone, even people you hadn't spoken to in years. After all, TrueVisage was a great way to break the ice and reconnect again, making it less awkward. Although I found it more awkward. I noticed on one of my close friend's page that there was a girl on his contact list who I had met years ago at his birthday dinner. We then met again at an Italian Food Festival; however, this had been well over ten years ago. We had been friends on Facebook, back when I first had an account, however when I closed down my original Facebook account, we lost touch. Here she was again and I thought this could be a good opportunity to reconnect.

I friended Clara immediately and waited patiently for her to (hopefully) accept. After just a few minutes I received a notification that she had accepted my friendship request. Step one complete. I replied and greeted her warmly with "long time no write!" and asked her how she was. She seemed pleased to hear from me and asked me what I was up to.

Chapter 20

This was it. My chance to introduce TrueVisage to someone on my list. I cast my mind back to what we had been taught. I didn't want to bombard her with the business all in one sitting. I had to play it cool and be nonchalant about it all. I was a Director of a successful business (more so in my mind than in reality). Relax and deep breath. I told Clara I was great, loving life and working from home. She replied back saying she wished she could work from home. It was as if my winning lottery ticket numbers had come through. I messaged back; this was the chance for me to home in on "her pain". I needed to find out what she wanted from life, what was making her unhappy and use this as a weapon. I replied back to Clara and began taking on a Therapist persona. I asked her how she was again and what she was doing for a living. She said she was a Personal Assistant, but hated her job. Yes! This was getting better and better. I asked her why she hated her job. She explained that she felt like a slave, her boss was horrible, she had been in various Personal Assistant roles for years and was sick of it. She also mentioned that she had recently purchased a home and had taken out a mortgage and that all the renovations were bleeding her income dry. Finally! All of my positive thinking and praying had come to fruition. This was an ideal sign up! It sickens me now to think that I was actually pleased to hear that someone was unhappy and that I would try to capitalise on their suffering.

I need to make money; therefore, my moral compass was non-existent at this point. Now it was my turn to empathise. I told Clara, that I too had been in a similar situation, that I hadn't been happy in my job and was sick of working for someone else. I didn't want to commute and wanted a way of earning an income which was flexible and fitted around my life.

Clara asked me what I was doing and not wanting to give too much away, I told her I had set up my own Beauty Business. Clara congratulated me and told me she had a certificate as a Masseuse. I told her that was great and said this would complement her skills perfectly! Hadn't she always dreamed of setting up her own Massage Business and being her own boss? She was hooked and wanted to know more. I told her I would send her a link which explained the business, I knew she was on her lunch break and didn't want to take up too much of her time, nor did I want to bombard her with too much information. I asked her for her personal email address and quickly scribbled it down. She also gave me her mobile number as I said I would touch base with her again in a day of so. Once I had finished, I congratulated myself on how well I had handled the call. I had ruthlessly worked on Clara's pain in order to find her Achilles Heel. I now shamefully look back and realised how awful my behaviour was.

Before TrueVisage, had I spoken to Clara and found out how unhappy she was with her job and financial situation, I would have felt sad for her and I would have sympathised, offering to help her with practical, realistic solutions. Instead I had been trained by TrueVisage to see her unhappiness as a way to profit, just like Sarah had done with me. I wasn't sad for Clara; her feelings didn't come into the equation. I was happy for me and what this could do for Linda Beauty. This is what MLM does to you. It makes you selfish and it makes you ruthless. You no longer view friends as friends or family as family. Everyone you know and meet becomes a potential customer, a potential sign up, a way of making money. If I spoke to my mum and she told me she was popping out to do her shopping, I would interject and remind her that I sold shampoo, hand cream and makeup.

If my sister complained about her skin: I would immediately recommend one of the TrueVisage products which would help. I couldn't just have a conversation without harping on about my business. I had changed and I couldn't see it then, but I look back now and see just how much it had affected me. My old self was slowly slipping away. It was great that I was so full of positivity and self-improvement, even though it was most of the time forced, however was I improving for myself or for TrueVisage? The positivity aspect was bordering on obsessive. I forbid myself to feel sad, angry or frustrated. It was a sign of weakness to process completely natural feelings and to deal with them in a healthy way. I was conditioned to view these thoughts as attracting negativity and as soon as I started showing an ounce of "negative" feeling, I quickly plastered a smile on my face and tried to think happy thoughts.

I was posting daily "positive quotes" on my Instagram page – "Live your best Life", "Keep going not matter how big the Mountain", "Positive Vibes Only", "Smile and the World Smiles with You"…On and on it went. I wasn't posting because I necessarily believed it, I was posting because I felt I had to, in order to get "likes" and to gain followers who could then become potential sign-ups. All the other TrueVisage clones were doing it, therefore I copied. We were taught to "Fish" on Social Media, to like someone's post, comment on it – wait until the person replies, then send them a Message. You didn't have to necessarily wait for a message, you could still message them regardless. If someone liked your post, you contacted them. All likes and comments were to be viewed as a potential sale or sign up. This is how we were taught to strike up relationships with a view to ensnaring people. Once upon a time, I had enjoyed using Instagram, now it was just a chore, a means to an end.

My obsession with all things positive even seeped into my relationship with James. If he came home from work and had had a bad day and just wanted to talk about it, I would immediately pounce on him, telling him to shed the negativity and think positively. He wasn't allowed to moan in the house, as far as I was concerned, our home was a negative free zone.

Most of the time James would indulge me and laughed it off, however I feel awful looking back now at the fact that I wasn't allowing him to simply be and recognise his feelings.

It had been two days and I reconnected with Clara. I made a point of timing my message with her lunch break so that she couldn't fob me off with being busy at work. She said she was popping out for a quick break and that she would call me once settled in the café close to her office.

I patiently waited for her call. When my phone rang, I took a deep breath and thought positive thoughts that this would be my first proper sign up. Clara sounded like she was in a good mood, she moaned for a bit about how crap her day had been and how much she hated her boss. I made a point of saying that all this could be over soon, should she choose to embark on the same journey as me. She said she definitely wanted to order some of the products, and that she thought opening up an account in order to take advantage of the discount seemed like a no brainer. She had watched the video I had sent her explaining the business model, however at this stage in her life, she didn't want to commit to working the business full time, as she was really bogged under with the renovations to her new home. I was a little deflated at this, however if she opened up an account I would still profit from her purchases. She said once the house was finished, around December, she would then consider committing to the business. For now, she would buy the products and if anyone asked her about what she was using, she would do as I did and get them to either buy or sign up. I could live with this, it was better than nothing!

I sent her the link and my TrueVisage UK ID code in order to link Clara to me and she promised she would sign up once she got home after work. As soon as I finished speaking with Clara I called Sarah with the good news. She was thrilled, however advised me to keep chipping away at Clara in order to get her to sign up people also and not to forget about how this was going to be her future business. Sarah also told me to get Clara to come to the St Alban meetings and join in on the weekly Zoom calls. She wanted me to also add Clara to the WhatsApp groups. I thought this was a bit hasty, after all, Clara was simply opening up an account to buy her own products, she didn't want to start up her business yet. According to Sarah, I had to begin wearing Clara down now and constantly remind her that this wasn't a hobby, it was a serious commitment. I reluctantly agreed, however I felt uncomfortable pressurising people. I ended the call and shrugged off the feeling of uneasiness I was beginning to feel. It was all negative and I needed to keep my vibes up.

I decided to contact the owner of the Gym again and ask her if she was still set for our date in March, she still seemed super keen and it was another potential sign up I could look forward to adding to my account. Despite my very slow start, things were beginning to look up and I felt super positive. I was still continuously reading self-help books about Network Marketing and Positive Mindset and religiously watching all of the TrueVisage Tutorial Videos on Facebook. Without realising it, every day that went by, I became more and more brainwashed.

Chapter 21

One day, I received a text message from Sarah, telling me that a live video was being streamed on Facebook that morning, from one of the super top earners, Steve. This man was in fact one of my Uplines and was so high up in the pyramid it was a miracle he didn't have clouds and birds rotating around his head.

The tutorial video was basically more brainwashing about how we needed to attract positivity and expel and negative thoughts. We had daily reminders on Facebook and on our WhatsApp groups and I of course now know the reason as to why I was actively encouraged to be part of them all. This was a guaranteed way for TrueVisage and all the top people to constantly pump their message into our minds in between all the meetings and events. Steve said that if our businesses were failing, if was because we were not trying and pushing hard enough. All blame lay out our door. However, here he was, saviour of the day with a video about how he grows his contacts on Facebook.

I leaned forward ready to take all advice onboard. Steve explained how he had created his very own excel sheet, which was linked to all of his contacts and would import all of their contacts address book on to your excel sheet. This would create an easy to use List, saving you time. Every time one of your contacts added someone to their address book, it would update your excel sheet. He then proceeded to work through a step by step lesson on how to create the sheet. He told us to do it whilst he showed us. It was mind bogglingly complicated. I listened and took notes, however I already had an excel sheet in place which I was happy (I use the word loosely, as I actually hated contacting people) to continue using and which already had lots of information on it I didn't want to lose.

Once he had finished his tutorial, he then went onto remind us all of the TrueVisage re-order points scheme which according to him, most of us were not taking advantage of.

He explained that we could sent up a monthly product re-order on our account, which would be automatically dispatched every month and we could earn points to spend on products. He advised we all set up four to five products to re-order (of course he did, he would profit immensely from this as well as all the other Uplines above me.) Sarah, messaged me afterwards to say she would help me to set this up. I logged off of Facebook and after three long attempts and two hours wasted at trying to set up the excel sheet, I decided I wouldn't bother, after all, I was my own boss and was happy to continue doing my thing and using my own excel sheet. I also thought it was wrong to simply help myself to other people's contacts, people I didn't know and contact them trying to push TrueVisage products onto them. I hadn't asked permission from my contacts and felt uncomfortable doing this.

I took stock of how far I had come so far; my friend had purchased a facial cleansing tool; my sister had purchased a mud mask. I had sold two bottles of hair growth shampoo to the family friend at the funeral. I had a potential sign up lined up, plus my meeting with the gym manager. I was hardly raking it in as I had been promised and had made in total less than £60 in commission. My out goings were way more as I had purchased a shed load of products to use on myself and to promote on social media. The main bulk of my commission had been from my friend buying the facial cleansing tool and I knew this was a one-off sale. In order to make the equivalent of what I had been earning in my job I would need to sell over seventy devices each month, which was never going to happen no matter how much positivity I emitted. I had to stay focused, I thought of all the other girls doing the same as me and that they were super successful. I needed to be patient and give it time. Things would begin to turn around soon.

Wednesday arrived and it was the day of my first Network Marketing meeting. I was really excited and felt super important and business like. I made my way over to the hotel and entered the restaurant area as directed in the email I received the previous week by the organisers. I was greeted by two gentlemen who were really friendly, along with their assistant. I was early, and was one of the first there, however I didn't mind as it gave me a chance to speak to them about the meeting format. They explained the running order for the next couple of hours. We usually waiting until everyone arrived and this was a chance to mingle. We then grabbed our breakfast and sat around the table in our designated area, we ate and chatted and it was all very relaxed. After we had finished eating, we each took it in turns to stand up and introduce ourselves and our businesses.

Each week, one of the attendees would then give a more detailed talk about what their business was about which would last about 20 minutes, and afterwards we would all swap business cards and people would then have the chance to talk to one and other in case someone's business or service was of interest. It was stressed however that we were not there to sell. If someone wanted to use your service or buy your product, they did this by contacting you afterwards. Whilst we were mingling pre-breakfast, I got chatting to a gentleman who was also part of a Multi-Level Marketing Company. His business revolved more around health supplements. He seemed really nice and had the same passion as me about positivity and the law of attraction. Once we had settled down and finished our breakfast, he was the first to introduce himself. As he spoke, I immediately began to feel a sense of Déjà vu. It was like being at the TrueVisage Success Summit and he repeated everything I had already heard. I wanted to interrupt and ask him if he had been to the same Success Summit as I had.

I was confused and couldn't work out how he knew all of the things I had heard at the TrueVisage events. He told his story about how he had been really ill and that after speaking to someone online, they recommended the supplement and it had changed his life. He vowed he would do the same and begin to sell the supplement. At the end of the meeting, just before I was about to leave, one of the meeting organisers approached me and asked if I had enjoyed the meeting and if I had found it useful. I had managed to hand out some of my cards and one of the ladies who ran her own travel agent was keen to buy a nail treatment product from me. I guess it had been useful. I asked about the Health Supplement chap and made a joke about how similar our business ethos was. The event organiser laughed and said that we were both working for MLM Companies and that both businesses were Pyramid schemes. He said that all this sort of thing originates for one place and uses the same formula. He said he probably shouldn't tell me this, however he felt sorry for the man, as he had been with the Health Supplement company for years and had spent a shed load of money, even racked up debt and made very little. The reason he stuck with it was because he truly believed what the Health Supplement Company Upline had told him, at that the supplement had helped in recover from his illness.

On my way home, I couldn't help thinking about what I had just heard. Surely, what he was doing was nothing like my experience. I choose to ignore what I had heard and concentrate on what I had lined up. There was a small niggle of doubt that was beginning to grow like a tiny shoot in my stomach, however I was getting used to nipping any negativity in the bud. My business wasn't going to grow if I let doubtful thoughts into my head. When I got home, I remembered that my Travel Agent contact was interested in buying a nail repair kit. This was a newly launched TrueVisage product and had been live for just over a week. I had been plugging it on Social Media for days with no luck – in fact, every Truvisage representative had been plugging it. According to what I was seeing and hearing, all the other girls were making a killing selling pack after pack. I was obviously doing something wrong, despite doing exactly what everyone else was doing. However, I finally had someone interested and I didn't want her keenness to buy to go cold. I also wanted to look into booking a holiday, therefore the whole process felt very much like "I scratch your back, you scratch mine".

I felt a little embarrassed about this new product as before it was launched we were told that TrueVisage were launching it in Australia and one of the girls from our WhatsApp group was off on a little holiday there and had promised that she could buy a bulk amount of packs at a super discounted price and sell them onto us at cost which was £27. I took up the offer and when I finally received it, thought it was absolutely rubbish. This product retailed at almost £45. It consisted of a cheap paper nail file with a buffer on one side and a file on the other and two pens. One which was a repair solution serum and one which was a nail protector. We were supposed to market it as the perfect product to use after gel manicures or acrylic nail removal.

I knew full well, that I purchase a similar file from any high street chemist of less that £3. A good nail oil and protector for less that £6-7 each. Therefore, I thought £45 was an absolute rip off – no wonder no one wanted to buy it! I messaged my Travel Agent contact with the details and gave her the retail price. She replied back saying that for that price it must be good! I then told her that if she opened up a TrueVisage account, she would be eligible the discount. She decided to opt for the account, I sent her the details, she set herself up and ordered the nail kit. At this point I should have been thrilled! I now had two official sign-ups – Clara and now my Travel Agent Friend. However, I hadn't really achieved anything, as neither person was signing up with the same idea as me – to start their own beauty business. My two sign-ups had done so, purely to save money on ridiculously expensive products.

As with all of the TrueVisage products, the packaging for the nail kit was cheap, flimsy and dated. I prayed that my Travel Agent customer wouldn't be annoyed when she received it. Sarah was calling me and messaging me daily. She was thrilled with my progress, and as our Gym meeting was fast approaching, she wanted to meet up to discuss how we were going to handle the meeting. She arrived at mine the following day, and we both settled down at my dining room table with our laptops. She asked me how I was getting on with setting up the contacts Excel sheet as per the tutorial on Facebook. I told her I wasn't going to bother with it, as it was super complicated, I had wasted hours trying to follow the tutorial and I was actually happy to use my own. Sarah face fell. She said that she was also having trouble with it, however was going to get it set up no matter how long it took as this was a super useful tool to boosting your business. I disagreed and said that I didn't like the idea of stealing and harassing other people's contacts, especially without asking permission first.

Sarah said she had a phone called lined up tomorrow with Chloe and apparently, Chloe was expecting Sarah to have the excel sheet set up. I was confused, why was Sarah fussed about what Chloe wanted, after all, we were our own bosses, Directors of our own businesses, Sarah didn't have to do what Chloe said. I voiced my opinion to Sarah, I could see she was feeling the pressure from Chloe, however she laughed it off and said she would get her husband to help her. Sarah said she had been telling Chloe all about me and how well I was doing, she had also told Chloe about our impending Gym meeting. Sarah gushed at how Chloe was really impressed with me and wanted to meet me for a coffee soon, along with Sarah. The way Sarah said it made me feel like I was getting an audience with some super important celebrity and that I should be honoured. I thought back to when Sarah had first introduced me to Chloe at my first St Albans meeting and she hardly batted an eyelid at me, now that I was potentially a good earner and would be bringing in lots of commission for her, I was suddenly deemed worthy of a meeting with her.

We moved on from our Chloe conversation and began planning our Gym meeting. The main product we would be touting was the Face Lift hand held device, however Sarah thought it would be good to bring some other product with us also, just in case the owner wanted to stock them. We didn't think the make-up range would be necessary, and opted more for the skincare products. I had my own stock, products I used, however Sarah said it would be wise to purchase several items to take with us, along with sample pots just in case. We agreed on the Body Tanning gel, Toothpaste, Mud Mask and the Serums for the Face Lift devise, in case we had to do a demonstration. I placed an order there and then with money I didn't really have, as I hadn't made any money and was dipping into our savings yet again. Sarah reassured me that this was a business investment and that if I secured the Gym owner as a client; I would be raking it in in no time. I guess it would look unprofessional to turn up empty handed or with half used products, so I clicked on the "buy" button and once again ignored the niggle of doubt in my gut.

I asked Sarah how business was going for her and she confidently said that it was great! She had a few orders ready to drop off to customers in the back of her car and would be leaving shortly so she could deliver them before the rush hour traffic. I couldn't help but wonder how the hell she was selling so much. No one wanted to buy the products from me, I had no enquiries and every time I looked on social media, I could see that many of the TrueVisage Reps wrote how their inboxes were full and that they were super busy dealing with orders. Sarah was the same. What was I doing wrong, was I being too negative? I also noticed pictures being posted of huge boxes full of TrueVisage products, which the girls would say were customer orders, ready for dispatching. I asked Sarah for advice – what was I doing wrong? Sarah simply shrugged her shoulders and told me that every one's journey is different. I was wrong to compare myself to others. She asked me if I had watched all the Facebook tutorials and if I was following all the advice on the TrueVisage website? I told her yes, I was plugging away every day without fail. She said that I needed to keep my vibes positive and that the universe would deliver in time. These weren't really the answers that I wanted. I couldn't see how sitting around sending messages to the universe was going to get me anywhere. Perhaps I was impatient. Perhaps I was too negative.

Maybe I did need to start being more cut throat and contacting strangers and cold calling.

Chapter 22

We had another St Albans meeting lined up and although in my heart I really didn't want to go I decided that I should attend and show my commitment. Maybe this was where I was going wrong. Not wanting to participate or keep the TrueVisage message fresh in my mind at all times was interfering with my positivity. I arrived at the hotel and grabbed a seat in the first row. All of the usual crowd was there and a few fresh-faced people ready to see what this new business opportunity was all about. The two group leaders, a husband and wife took the stage and ran through the business plan. We also had the usual testimonials. Half way through one, Sarah leaned over and whispered to me if I wanted to stand up and give a testimonial. I was a little horrified as being caught off guard and I hadn't prepared anything. She told me to be natural and subtly pointed to me and to the head speaker, indicated that I was next to stand up. I awkwardly took the stage and said my name and why I was now a TrueVisage Rep – or rather, Director of my own business.

When I look back now, I realise that I basically sounded like everyone else. My "story" was exactly like all the other TrueVisage Reps. I was a clone. I harped on about positivity, expelling negative energy, working at it and doing everything that TrueVisage recommends. I stood on that stage and convinced myself that I was happy, when in actual fact I had completely screwed up my life. I had left my job, yes, I wasn't happy, however it was paying me good money and I could have kept at it until I found something else. I was my own person with my own identity. I had interests and hobbies; I had a life. Okay, so it wasn't perfect, but it was still *good*. Instead now, I was unemployed, pretending to be a Director, hanging around with people I had nothing in common with, apart from TrueVisage. I had no money coming in, I was lonely all day at home, on my own. I was plugging away constantly on social media peddling crap products which no one wanted to buy. I was constantly pretending that my life was great, I was trying to convince people that I was living my best life when in actual fact I wasn't. It was all lies. A pretence. Fake it till you make it. I found having to be super positive all of the time when my life was anything but draining.

Having to invent things to post about, so that my boring time indoors or in the coffee shop looked interesting on Social Media. Pleasing complete strangers and trying to accumulate "likes" on line from people I didn't know or care about in order to feel complete was depressing.

However, I stood on that stage and told people how wonderful being part of TrueVisage was. I told them that I now had freedom, I was successful, I was making new friends, I was the boss of my own business and called all the shots. And looking back now I realise; this was what everyone else was doing. They were lying. They were lying in order to get people to sign up. They were brainwashed into thinking that this was good, that this was what you had to do. If you admitted the truth, you were a failure. You had failed yourself, your business and your family. I left the stage and made my way back to my seat realising I had just done what I had seen at my very first meeting. We were all liars and we did it to trap people into signing up. The saying "misery loves company" springs to mind.

We finished the meeting with the reminder video that we all needed to book our tickets for the big Success Summit in Spain. The same video which was shown at the January Success Summit was played again, showing us all how amazing the European Summit was. It was Sun, Sea, Glitz and Glamour – a trip which would boost our business. I still hadn't committed to it and Sarah wanted to know if I was going.

It was a huge expense and although James said I could use the savings, I still felt bad about it, however I really didn't want to miss it. Everyone would be there, all the top earners and key speakers who would give us more tips on how to work the business and make it a success. It would also be a fantastic thing to plug on social media as an Attraction Marketing tool in order to tempt people into joining. This was the life we led, successful business people, swanning off to Europe on business trips with other likeminded success business people. I promised Sarah I would speak with James again and give her a definite answer tomorrow. Sarah still hadn't booked her flight of hotel and kept on saying that if I went, we could travel and stay in the same hotel together. This did make me feel a little bit pressured, however I also felt flattered that she wanted us to go together. When I got home, I mentioned the trip again to James and as I expected, he was still on board about me going.

He was still really supportive and knew deep down that I didn't want to miss out on the trip. The next morning, I messaged Sarah so say I would be going. I told her that James and I had saved quite a few British Airways points and that as a treat, I could book us Business Class seats for just £150 each return. We would only be paying the taxes on the flight. The only snag was that flight times and availability meant that we would need to leave in the afternoon on Sunday and would miss out on the White Tie Gala Dinner, which was the finale to the weekend. I wasn't too bothered, as I didn't have an outfit and knew that buying a dress and shoes would just be another expense and the whole gala dinner thing wasn't my scene. There would be a big party on the Saturday night and this was enough for me. Sarah, I think was a little bit disappointed and I said she could always book a seat with another airline and I would meet her there and she could fly back on Monday, however she didn't want to travel alone.

She told me that she had never travelled by herself and didn't want to risk getting lost or miss the flight back. I then said I would look into the hotel, as Sarah mentioned sharing a room with the other girls, however I really wanted privacy. I was of course happy to share with Sarah, as I knew we were similar in the sense that we were both quiet and liked to relax, not major drinkers or party people. Sharing with two or three other women with one bathroom didn't appeal to me. I also wanted to avoid staying in a hotel full of

TrueVisage reps. I knew it would be noisy and after each day, I wanted to retreat to somewhere a little bit quiet. Sadly, I had left it a little late and all of the hotels in the centre, close to the Summit venue had been booked up. The event was being held in a small, coastal town (which I had never hear of) and it seemed that thousands would be attending the event from all over the world. Sarah had been promised a place with a group of girls sharing in an Air BnB, however she really wanted to stay with me. I finally found a hotel approximately a thirty-minute walk from the venue. It wasn't ideal, as we would have to take a taxi or bus, especially in the evenings, however it was clean, modern and it had a pool. It was also reasonably priced. I reserved the room and Sarah was pleased that plans were now firmly in place.

She owed me £245 in total for the booking and she promised me she would pay me as soon as possible. Apparently, the last couple of months had been quiet on the business front so she didn't have the spare funds. I reassured her that there was no rush, I had already paid for everything and purchased my event ticket at £250. She could re-pay me once business picked up. As our Gym meeting was coming up soon, Sarah asked me if I had purchased the Face Lift device. I hadn't really thought about it and knew that Sarah owned one, therefore I hoped I could use hers for the demonstration. When I asked Sarah if I could use hers, she told me that her device wasn't working very well and the last thing she wanted was to drive all the way to Essex and then be unable to get the gadget working. My heart sank at the prospect of purchasing the device as it cost over £250, this was minus the £30 for the serums. I had already spent over £200 on products to take along to meeting and just couldn't afford another £250. I wasn't making any money and this would be yet another loan from our savings. I explained this to Sarah and she said she had a solution.

She had an extra device which she had originally purchased for one of her customers. They had let her down and she ended up stuck with it, as she had left it too late to return it back to the TrueVisage customer service office for a refund. She was happy to sell it to me for £100, however it didn't have a warranty or box, however she assured me it was brand new. It was a good saving and I really needed the device to showcase to the Gym owner. I agreed to purchase it from Sarah, seeing as she owed me the money for the Spain trip, I would simply deduct it from that. Sarah agreed and I felt relieved. I had saved some money and could use this devise to create a video to could post on my social media.

At one of the meetings I had attended we were told to create online videos of us using the products. We were told that videos made you seem more "real" to your followers, which would help to build trust which in turn would lead to more sales. I was posting videos regularly and still had received no queries or sales regarding the products. To add to my deflation, a friend of mine messaged me one day to tell me that TrueVisage products were being openly sold on Amazon and eBay for a fraction of the price that we sold them for. I couldn't tell if the online sellers were official TrueVisage representatives or not. This was strictly forbidden as part of our TrueVisage contract and I immediately messaged our group chat to find out if the other girls knew about the breach of contract. One of the senior Uplines messaged back saying that unfortunately this does happen, however to ignore it as the products were fake. I thought that was strange, as who the hell would want to create counterfeit TrueVisage products?? I mean, they were hardly a sought-after designer brands. Everyone I approached had never heard of TrueVisage, I had never heard of them until I was introduced by Sarah! I found out the painful truth when I left, that these were people who had also left TrueVisage and were trying to claw back money by selling their surplus stock which they were unable to return back to head office. They were breaking the Terms and Conditions as they had no other way to shift the products. Luckily, I never had to do this. However, at the time, I believed what I was told and thought that this was simply a case of people breaking the rules or criminals exploiting the business.

Chapter 23

It was the day of my gym meeting and I was excited at the prospect of this being a commercial client – finally my big break! Sarah arrived at 10am, and as I got into the car, she said she needed to pop past a petrol station to fill up the car. She once again hinted to me that business had been slow and that money was tight and that although she didn't mind giving me the lift to Essex, the trip would cost her in petrol. I felt the conversation taking an awkward turn and offered to of course pay for the petrol. I didn't mind, I mean, I had absolutely no earnings coming in and was relying on James and our savings, however I felt that I should at least offer to pay for fuel. It did annoy me slightly, as although Sarah kept on saying that the Gym owner would be my client, she would still profit from her as she was my Upline. I'm not the sort of person to argue over money, and didn't want an atmosphere in the car, so graciously took the fuel cost on the chin – yet another business expense I suppose. Sarah often hinted that she had bestowed the gift of TrueVisage onto me, which left me feeling like I was indebted to her.

It was a long journey and once on the motorway, the conversation of course turned to TrueVisage and Sarah and I bounced positive vibes off of each other. We of course agreed that business was slow and that we weren't earning much, but this was part and parcel of being a business owner. This was the first proper time Sarah had admitting to struggling financially. I reminded her of our first conversation, when she had introduced me to the business, she said she was making her salary equivalent of over £2000 per month. She seemed to shift uncomfortably in her seat and said that the £2000 earnings weren't guaranteed every month. She told me that some months were good, others were bad. It felt like Sarah was confident enough with me to admit the truth. She opened up about her sister-in-law's and how she had fallen out with them over

TrueVisage. She offered them the business opportunity and they declined. Sarah thought that they were snobs, constantly complaining that they were broke, but too proud to take on TrueVisage as a way of earning extra cash. She now hardly spoke to them, as according to Sarah, they were they typical negative family members we were warned about at the Success Summits - Dream Stealers that we need to cut out of our lives.

We arrived at the gym and met with the owner, Cathy. She was lovely and really open to using the Face Lift Device in her spa rooms. Sarah and I sat down in her office and proceeded to show Cathy the products we thought she might like to stock in her gym. When I had spoken to Cathy over the phone, she had given me the impression that she wanted to do this, however during our meeting she completely changed her mind - all she really wanted to do was use the Face Lift Device. She also forgot to mention to me that she already had a device which had been purchased years ago by the previous owner and left in the stock cupboard. It still worked and all Cathy really needed were the serums.

I felt completely deflated. Weeks and weeks of planning, calls and emails during which I had been given the impression that I would be signing up a high earning customer, now looked like being a small commission earner. Cathy explained that she was running a charity fashion show at the gym in the coming weeks and that she wanted us to show case the Face Lift Device, giving people Face Lifts with the proceeds going to charity. We could charge £5 to £10 per facial, all proceeds going to the chosen charity. So, this was what this was all really about, we were only really needed to work at the charity party. Cathy was lovely, but I couldn't help feel that all this had been a complete waste of time. I had patiently waited weeks to finally meet and she only really wanted us to run a stall at her event. I of course wanted to support the charity, I thought it was a great idea – but at the time I was so driven to build my business and desperate to make money, that this was ultimately my top priority.

I explained to Cathy that if she wanted to use the Device, she would need to purchase the serums. I said she could of course buy them from me at the retail cost or open up a wholesale account. I explained the benefits of this and said that she could also run a side gig of selling products to clients. Cathy explained that this wasn't what she wanted to do. She would simply open up the wholesale account to buy serums. Cathy was now my third sign up, however none of my sign-ups were wanting to expand and sign people up, therefore I stood to make a small commission just on their personal purchases. They would not attend meetings, group calls and were not interested in building a business.

I felt like I was getting nowhere. I was investing so much time, money and effort into signing people up and in truth, it just wasn't worth it. I should have been pleased at the outcome of the meeting, and on the journey home Sarah drilled in the message of positive thinking and how everything would fall into place. She asked me to attend one of her network marketing groups the next day. I had been back to my local Wednesday meetings a few times and although everyone was lovely, it was just the same people there each week, which just seemed pointless. Apart from my Travel Agent contact, who had only purchased the Nail Repair Kit, I had no other interest from the meeting. I needed a fresh group of people to pitch to, was there much point seeing as Sarah was part of the meeting also? Everyone there would already know about TrueVisage – if no one was signing up with Sarah, why would they sign up with me? I declined the offer, as quite frankly, I couldn't afford the wasted petrol and I wanted to stay home and focus on a plan to boost sales. I shouldn't be disheartened. I needed to keep positive and remember TrueVisage's main message. If the business is failing, it's down to me and my attitude. The gym situation was just another blip and I should make the best of the charity event, as I may well get some sign-ups on the night! Every cloud has a silver lining after all.

Just before we left Sarah reminded me to take a photo of the outside of the gym and post a quick story onto my Instagram about our visit. She recommended I caption it with something along the lines of "spending the day with another new customer – expanding my business in Spa and Beauty Rooms – great Gym collaboration!". It was all phony, but once again, this was the sort of exaggeration which was condoned and which everyone seemed to be doing as a way of attraction marketing. These were the lies which were used to entice people into signing up. None of it was real, we faked it till we made it. Four years in and Sarah was doing this and I had fallen for it. On the journey home, Sarah once again opened up to me and said that her husband, Max, had also spoken to her about perhaps looking for a job. I asked Sarah if things were really that bad for her and if her TrueVisage business wasn't doing so well anymore. She of course didn't want me to know the truth and explained that it wasn't always the case that she earned £2,000 a month, despite the fact that she had told me the opposite when we had first spoken. Sarah however refused to go back to working for someone else. In the TrueVisage community, having a "normal" job was seen to be something to be embarrassed about. It meant you had failed in life and were giving up.

You were constantly encouraged to brag so much on social media about how you were living your best life, you culled everyone who loved and cared for you and surrounded yourself with TrueVisage clones, that anyone who had been doing this business for years felt that if they simply stopped, what would they go back to? They had no job, no friends, other than TrueVisage "friends", chances are they had broken most of their family relationships. They had no doubt alienated most of the people they knew. They had been bragging to everyone that their life was so great, if they then stopped, how would they rebuild their old life? TrueVisage cleverly sets you up to surround yourself with everything TrueVisage related that you become a shell of your former self. Do this for a full year, two years, three, four, five….and it becomes harder and harder to break away.

You begin to believe the bullshit. You have no option but to keep going with the lie in the hope that one day, you will become a success like all of the people at the very top of the pyramid (which is a miniscule percentage).

James was at home when I arrived back and I told him about the gym meeting. He said it was still a good sign that I would earn from the serum sales. He then went quiet and gave me a serious look. James said that perhaps I should give it until Christmas and if I was still not making any real money, I should perhaps think about stopping and finding a proper job. This was something I had been dreading, the leaders at TrueVisage had warned us about unsupportive partners. James was crushing my dream of being my own boss, being free from the nine to five rat race. He was giving me a time limit to prove myself. I felt pressured. I had worked so hard and invested so much. I had been reading books about positive thinking every day, I had participated in all of the Zoom calls, attended all of the meetings. I had replaced all of my beauty and skincare products with TrueVisage products. I was posting every day on social media. I was cold calling and emailing people daily. All of my efforts were going into my business and now James was telling me that I only had till the end of the year to prove myself.

I was angry and upset, however didn't want to attract negativity into my space and I simply agreed with him to keep the peace. I would prove I could do it and gloat once I was picking up my pin title on stage at next year's Success Summit. I went upstairs and immediately message the group telling them what James had said. I was hit with a barrage of messages all commiserating with me about how unfair James was behaving. One of girls said she heard about one woman who had left her husband as he was so negative and unsupportive. I thought this was a bit extreme, I mean yes, I was annoyed with James, however I wasn't going to divorce him over TrueVisage. I laughed off her message, however her response was grave. She said that ultimately, our loyalty was to the business and we had to do whatever it took to make it a success. She then sent me the link to the TrueVisage Tutorial which focused on unsupportive friends and relatives – "watch this Hun, it will make you realise".

I clicked on the link and watch the short video. It was an American actor, posing as a husband, clutching a laundry basket and speaking to the camera whilst he was doing the family laundry. He explained to viewers that he wasn't onboard with his wife when she first mentioned TrueVisage. He thought it was a waste of time and didn't think his wife would stick with it. He didn't support her at first, until he went to one of the meetings. He was blown away by the support and business model. He knew it made his wife happy and realised that a "happy wife, meant a happy home". He began helping out at home more and doing his fair share in looking after the kids, so that his wife would have time to build the business. In fact, his wife is doing so well and making so much money that the husband told us that he is now thinking of joining TrueVisage too. He was sceptical at first, however now he really thinks it's great. He didn't want to lose his wife, therefore thought it was wise to be open minded and support her.

The video was weird and totally staged. In the back of my mind however, I wanted James to give me more time and support me more. I wasn't going to be bullied into giving up my business and kept the link in case I needed to show him the video.

Chapter 24

The following day, I was up early as usual and headed out for a swim, making sure I posted a short video of me walking to the gym in the sunshine in order to brag about how much freedom this business allowed me so that I could take time out to lounge about at the pool. I decided that today I would I pop into London to visit my parents. I could post more snippets online about how great my life was, not being stuck behind a desk all day long. I would perhaps do a little window shopping and treat myself to a manicure (I couldn't justify the expense, but it was another great post for my Instagram feed). I grabbed an early afternoon train, posting once again online about how working this business meant I didn't need to ask my boss for time off. I was lucky enough to be my own boss babe and could work my business while on the train. This was of course absolute rubbish. I wasn't working anything, other than posting lies online in order to attract people into doing the same.

I alighted at Highbury and Islington Station in North London and thought it would be nice to walk along Upper Street. It was nice to be away from the laptop, The List, from the cold calls and emails and from having to think about TrueVisage – for just that short time, I felt like my old self again, carefree and window shopping. I walked into one of my favourite clothes shops and thought it would be nice to check out their new seasons collection, perhaps a little treat for the Spain Success Summit. I picked out a few pieces to try on and one of the sales-assistance walked me to a free changing cubicle. The boutique was quiet and as I was trying on the clothes, the sales assistant was happy to stand outside and talk to me.

Her accent seemed really familiar and I established that she was Italian, in fact she from a small town close to where my parents were from in Sicily. She had been living in London for two years, and had come to the UK in order to improve her English and to hopefully build a life in London. Her name was Francesca. We talked about Italy, food and eventually the conversation moved towards what I did for a living. She asked me if I had the day off from work and I told her that I ran my own business. She was in awe of me and said that I was lucky to be my own boss. At this stage, I had paid for a couple of items and we were standing by the tills. The boutique was still quiet and it seemed like she was the only person on duty, therefore she was happy to have the company and we continued to chat away.

I gave her the run-down of my story. TrueVisage advises all of its representatives to have a story – this is the reason why you decided to go into the business and is what you tell people – it's your rags to riches tale. My story was that I had been unhappy in my old job, I was "tired of being tired" and wanted more out of life. I was sick of commuting into London, doing the same thing, day in and day out and that I craved a change going into my forties. I wanted to be my own boss and call the shots going forward. I wanted to earn money for myself as opposed to making someone else rich. I was introduced to the business by a trusted family member, who was living the dream and who wanted to gift me this amazing opportunity. I took a leap of faith and was now living the same dream and living my best life. It really was that simple.

The story is devised so as not to give too much away. This is simply to entice people into wanting to know more. It worked, as once I had finished, Francesca immediately asked me what it was that I did. At this point, I wanted to keep her intrigued, I told her that I had to dash off to meet someone and that it she gave me her email and mobile number, I would send her the information later on this evening. Once again, drawing from the training at the Success Summit and the TrueVisage Facebook tutorials, we were told we should never leave a prospective sign up without obtaining their contact details. She grabbed a piece of scrap paper from behind the counter and wrote down her details. It had been nice speaking to her and she told me she was keen to know more, especially after I gave her one of my business cards and she saw that my business related to beauty. I left the boutique feeling positive that I could have met yet another sign-up, one who by the sounds of it, could be a proper business sign up who wants to actually start a business. It helped that she was Italian also, as she would have contacts in Italian she could sign up and sell to.

One of the good things about TrueVisage was that it was a global business and was operating in forty other countries. I had already approached family and friends in Italy; however, no one was interested. I'll admit, this really frustrated me. I couldn't understand why no one wanted to do this. Despite the fact that I wasn't doing well I was blinded by this and could only see the benefits, the potential to earn extra money, the positivity, the ease of running a business from your phone. I was beginning to take on the same attitude as Sarah in that I had family and friends who would constantly moan that they were broke, yet didn't want to take on a business opportunity that could earn them an extra income and make them a success. It wasn't yet working for me; however, I was sure it would in time and I was sure it would work for others as I had proof from all of the other successful women and men doing it. I had never met them and didn't really know them; however, I had been hardwired to believe them.

I was annoyed that none of my family and friends wanted to support me and was beginning to develop a resentful attitude. I of course never voiced this, however deep down I looked forward to the day when I would be earning a huge amount of money and could gloat about it to all of the non-believers. This was another message TrueVisage instilled into our brains, that one day we would be able to show all of the haters and non-believers our success, until then, we faked it till we made it.

I left the boutique and made my way to a nail bar I knew would be quiet as it was a mid-week afternoon and I was sure there would be no other customers inside. I was right, it was quiet and I was reassured by the super helpful nail technician that I didn't need an appointment. Once I was comfortably sat down, the nail technician,

Nina, asked me if I was off work for the day. Once again, as I had done with Francesca, I explained that I was my own boss and had decided to take the day off to pamper myself a little. I was met with the same reaction, of how lucky I was and that Nina too wished she could work for herself. I felt like the Universe was finally answering my prayers and that Nina could now be yet another potential sign up.

I regaled her with my story and also decided to throw in my meeting with Francesca who was chomping at the bit to sign up (this was an exaggeration, however I thought there was no harm on adding a little "fear of missing out" factor to the tale). Nina had actually heard of TrueVisage and had used the Whitening Toothpaste years ago. She seemed to remember that it was good (although I wanted to contradict her with my opinion, I kept my mouth shut as I didn't want to put her off!) and was happy to buy one from me. As I did with everyone I spoke to, I offered her the opportunity to open up a wholesale account. I told Nina that she could buy herself a toothpaste and recommend it to her colleagues who could then buy from her. Why not make some money in the process? She agreed and could see the money earning potential. Finally! A trip to London had resulted in two potential sign-ups, things were looking up!

As with Francesca, I asked Nina for her contact details and gave her one of my business cards. She asked me if I had a website to which I answered "no" – we used the TrueVisage website, however Nina's question gave me a little light bulb moment and made me wonder if whether a website was perhaps something I needed to explore in order to grow my business. None of the other girls had websites, no one else was using this tool and I thought that perhaps I could be the first to explore this avenue. I told Nina I would send her more information on how to open up an account as well as the link to the business model video.

I left the nail bar with a spring in my step – I was pleased with how my day had gone. Pounding the pavement and talking to people face to face was obviously that way to go. It seemed that strangers were more willing to open up and listen when you were directly in their presence as opposed to at the end of the phone or email. I decided this was how I was going to work my business going forward. I felt positive and couldn't wait to get home to begin developing plans for a website.

My visit to mum and dads was brief. They asked me how I was and how the business was doing. I explained that all was well and that it took time to build up client relationships. I mentioned the potential sign up of Francesca and Nina and that I already had two other sign-ups, one of which was a business. My parents were pleased and I put on the pretence that things were going well. I didn't tell them that I had made no money. I told them also about the trip to Spain and that I had a good feeling about the months ahead. I don't think they took what I was doing seriously, at one point my dad asked me if I was going to get a job soon. On the train journey home, I shook my head at them both, my parents didn't understand and their lack of belief simply spurred my on to make this a success and prove them wrong.

Chapter 25

The next day, I had my usual morning catch up over the phone with Sarah. She was excited about my news regarding Francesca and Nina. I had sent them emails the previous evening containing all of the information they needed to set themselves up with wholesale accounts. Francesca hadn't replied, however Nina said she would set herself up as soon as she had some spare time. I made a note to chase them up a day or two.

I mentioned my website idea to Sarah. I wanted to create a website showcasing the TrueVisage products I used, giving my customer the chance to purchase via the website. I wanted to design it with my own personal review of the products, perhaps incorporating a little bit about me, my story and a beauty blog. Sarah told me that the idea was good, however I wouldn't be able to directly sell the TrueVisage products from the website or show the logo or name of the products on the site. This would be a breach of our contract. I would have to photograph the products covering the logo and name and I wouldn't be able to list the product name either. I was beginning to realise why no one else was doing this, however I was determined not to let all of the rules set me back. I thought the idea of a website was really good and that it would give me an edge over everyone else. I was also desperate for something creative to work on during the day as I was becoming bored at home on my own with nothing else to do.

Sarah asked me how I was getting on with Cathy, the Gym Owner. I told her that she had placed an order for just one box of serums to be used at the charity event. Sarah told me that she would need to order more as there was just three applications per box, which would mean that we could only perform three demonstrations. In truth, I lacked the energy to deal with Cathy. It was really difficult to get hold of her and when she did finally call me back, she was always in a rush, I felt having Cathy as a sign up was not worth the hassle. I thought in the beginning that she was going to be a big earner, however the impression that I got was that she simply wanted us to be another stall holder at her charity fashion show. It just wasn't worth the trip all the way to Essex and the hassle of constantly chasing her up. I voiced this to Sarah and she said I had the wrong attitude. Sarah was convinced that we would blow everyone away with the fabulous Face Lift Device at the gyms charity event and that Cathy would want to buy more products from me.

In truth, I thought the device was an absolute con. Sarah and popped round before our gym meeting to show me how the device worked. I was going to have a half face demo so that I could see the difference. I had seen videos of the results from the device on the TrueVisage Facebook before and after databank and was amazed at the results. Videos of women having half face facials, showing the half of the face which had had the treatment looking ten years younger. I was amazed at why this device wasn't stocked in shops and beauty salons. I then experienced the facial myself, only to see absolutely no difference in my skin or face – the half which had had the facial looked and felt no different, despite Sarah telling me I looked great. Before posting the pictures onto my social media, she told me to apply a filter and so that my skin would look a little brighter. I also had to position my face a certain way and she applied some face app to the photo also. None of the image was real and I realised that this was what all of the girls were doing to their photos, a re-touch here and there in order to post the best "results". It wasn't the products which were making your skin look fabulous, it was the filters and face editing apps. My eyes were being opened to a world of lies and deceit and the more and more I experienced, the less and less I wanted to be a part of it.

I ended the phone call with Sarah and decided that working on designing a website was the next step forward for my business. I wanted to begin branching out on my own and to be less dependent on Sarah. I knew she was my Upline and that she would profit from my sales, however I wanted to begin building my own team and I convince myself I could nurture Clara, Cathy, Francesca and Nina.

I spent a solid five days working on creating my website. I took photos of the TrueVisage products I used and uploaded them to the site along with personal reviews of the products. I was careful not to name the product and I covered up the TrueVisage logo. At the bottom on each product, I simply added a line that if anyone wished to order, they simply needed to contact me. This would hopefully lead people to purchasing or if I was really lucky, signing up to the businesses. I was really pleased with my efforts and was proud with myself for creating my very own website. It was a small cost; however, I was hoping to reap the rewards, and it also looked a little more professional on my social media having a link to my own website. I decided I would add a personal and beauty blog too.

During the time I was working my website, Nina (the nail technician) had opened up a wholesale account and ordered the Whitening Toothpaste and Mud Mask and she promised to promote these on her Instagram. I hadn't heard from Francesca, the sales assistant. After several messages, she finally responded telling me that she wasn't interested. I decided to focus my attention on Nina, as she seemed keen to sell products also and I arranged to meet with her on her day off to explain the business to her in more detail and to introduce her to Sarah.

My website had been live for just a few days and I received an email enquiry for a potential customer wanting to know if the products I was reviewing were tested on animals. This was super tricky question and had been covered at the training day of the January Success Summit. We were told to tell people that the products were not tested on animals, however some of the pharmaceutical products such as the supplements were manufactured in countries where animal testing was allowed, therefore we couldn't guarantee that the products were not tested on animals. We were also told to laugh the question off with "I am not responsible for making the products, I just sell them". I thought this sounded really unprofessional and seeing as these were products which we were promoting, we should at least be able to tell our potential clients how they were produced. I replied back to the query with a more subtle response, which was based around the template we were given and I was not surprised when I didn't hear back from the person again. I loved my website and I enjoyed adding to it, however sadly, I received no sales or sign-ups from it, after all, who in their right mind is going to buy a product which has its name and logo constantly hidden from view. Who would trust a stranger who is a business owner yet constantly cagey about their product of business? Once a customer finds out what the product is, they no doubt search for it on Amazon or eBay and find that they can purchase it for a fraction of the price. I had obstacle after obstacle put in front of me and I was still wondering how all of the successful, top earners were making money.

Chapter 26

Sarah messaged the group WhatsApp announcing that she was hosting a Pamper Party at her home and she wanted us all to attend. I had heard about these Pamper Parties and most of the girls had hosted them. This was simply a way to sell products to friends and family at your home whilst adding some food, wine and music to the event to make it feel less like a sales pitch. I was actually thinking of hosting my own, therefore I thought going to Sarah's would be a good way to get an idea of how this sort of thing was hosted. My friends and family were not interested in the products or my business when I posted online, however if I could showcase a selection of products for them to actually *try*, it could be enough to sway them. My cousin had asked about trying the lip gloss and if I could get my hands on a selection of colours for her, she might buy from me.

Sarah's Pamper Party was being held on a Friday evening. Julia, Sarah's mother would be attending also and kindly offered to give me a lift. Julia picked me at 7pm and as she was driving, she asked me how the business was going. I felt I had to tread carefully, as I didn't want to say the wrong thing to her. The little seed of doubt had been growing in my mind and try as I might to suppress it, it reared its ugly head from time to time. I tried to stay positive and said that it was a slow process, however Sarah reassured me that things would fall into place and I of course trusted her as she was family and had gone through the same process herself.

Julia glanced over at me and said that she worried about Sarah. As her mother, Julia of course supported Sarah and knew TrueVisage made her happy, however she felt Sarah simply needed to get proper job and perhaps run the TrueVisage gig on the side. I was surprised at hearing this as I thought Sarah was earning a steady income from her TrueVisage sales and sign-ups. At this point, Julia realised she had perhaps said too much and changed the subject. She was relieved that Sarah and I were travelling to the Spain Success Summit together and thought Sarah would be in good hands with me there with her.

We arrived at Sarah's house and once inside, I noticed a couple of girls there from our St Albans gatherings. I didn't know anyone else there, however as Sarah introduced me to everyone, I quickly established that they were all her neighbours and some relatives from Julia's side. Everyone was chatting away, and I noticed Sarah had a very small selection of TrueVisage Products on display in her living room. It hardly seemed worth it; the selection was so small. Some people were looking at the products and trying them. Sarah had been absent for quite a while and I asked one of the girls where she was. Apparently, Sarah had arranged for a Tarot Card Reader to read our cards upstairs and was giving the lady our names, and allocating a time slot to us all. I wasn't keen on the idea and thought it was a waste of time. I had had my cards read once, years ago during a holiday with James in New York. He thought it would be a laugh. Needless to say, that pretty much everything the Tarot Card Reader had said was wrong. She said my husband and I would have up to four children and to this day, my husband and I are childfree. When I told her, we were definitely not having kids, she changed the prediction to dogs. She also said I liked to travel, which was glaringly obvious seeing as we were on holiday.

Sarah appeared in the living room and excitedly announced that we had all been designated a 30-minute slot with her Tarot Card Reader friend. However, the reading would cost us £10 each. I was annoyed that she had assumed we would all want our cards read; everyone was happy about it and I didn't want to come across as a penny pincher. The evening was well under way and one by one, we all disappeared upstairs, as each woman came down, they looked excited at having had a super positive future ahead of them. Of course, everyone there representing TrueVisage had been told that their future was full of success and I had a sneaky suspicion that the same prediction lay ahead for me.

It was finally my turn to go upstairs, I walked into the bedroom and was met by a middle-aged woman, sat at a small round table positioned at the end of the bed. The lights were dimmed low and a scattering of candles flickered around room. The Tarot Card Reader greeted me and asked me to take a seat. She gave me the deck of cards and asked me to shuffle them until I felt ready to hand them back to her. I shuffled for a minute or two, we sat in silence, and while I was looking at the cards, I could feel her looking at me. I gave the cards up and she asked me to split the desk into eight small piles. She then took two cards from the top of each deck.

She lay the cards face up and these were now my cards which she would read. I knew, as soon as the Tarot Card Reader began talking that Sarah had already briefed her on everything. It was ridiculously obvious. The Reader mentioned that I had started a "new journey" in my life, I was now on the road to success. I was about to enter into a new phase in my new business, about to sign a contract of some sort or enter into an agreement with a business associate (meaning the Gym). I would be traveling soon to an important destination which would be the turning point in my career (Spain Success Summit). I tried not to look frustrated at having parted with £10 which was no doubt being split between this woman and Sarah. For all I knew, the Tarot Card Reader was probably a TrueVisage Representative, here to convince us that we needed to stick with the business, as we were all heading for "success".

I won't bore you with the full reading, however as we came to the end – I felt like I had been taken for a fool that evening. This Pamper Party was just a staged meeting, during which we had been duped into the card reading simply to dispel any negative doubts and cement that fact we all needed to keep going with our businesses – all under the guise of an innocent card reading. After my reading had finished, I made my way downstairs and was immediately met with a barrage of questions from everyone all wanting to know what had been predicted for me. I didn't say much as I pretended that by telling them, my future wishes wouldn't come true – the truth was I couldn't be bothered to be part of the pretence.

I decided that evening that I was going to host my own Product Launch (I refused to call it a Pamper Party, as that sounded too childish). I was going to take it seriously and hopefully get lots of people to attend. As I was putting on my coat, Sarah approached me and asked if our meeting with Nina had been arranged. We needed to begin coaching her on how to start up her business. I had been in touch with Nina and she had a day off soon and was happy to meet up for a coffee close to where she lived in London. The latest update I had had from Nina was that she had ordered the Whitening Toothpaste and Mud Mask and that after a post on her Instagram, a couple of her colleagues had asked her about the Toothpaste and she had placed an order for some. She seemed positive about the immediate orders and I was happy for her. It had made me a small commission; however, I was worried that bombarding Nina at this early stage might scare her off. Sarah didn't agree with me and said we needed to strike while the iron was hot.

Chapter 27

I finalised the details of our meeting with Nina and Sarah and I made our way to a small coffee shop in London on a bright Wednesday morning. I thought Sarah being present wasn't a good idea, as Nina didn't know her and I felt like we were almost strong arming her into TrueVisage, however Sarah said she needed to be present in case Nina had any doubts, as she had been with TrueVisage longer than I had, and would be a reassuring presence. Sarah and I arrived early, ordered our coffees and I noticed I picked up the bill again, as I did every time we went out, as Sarah seemed to distance herself from the till each time. For someone making lots of money, she never seemed to want to spend any.

We made our way to the seating area upstairs and as we sat down, I received a text from Nina telling me that she was five minutes away. I messaged back, saying we were sat upstairs. Sarah warned me not to give too much away about the business and to let her do the talking, Nina came into view and I waved her over. The greeting was a little bit awkward, as I didn't really know her that well, having only met her once and having exchanged just a few messages via Instagram. Sarah was all ease and friendliness and kept on calling her "Hun" and exclaiming how amazing it was that she was now doing this business with us. Nina looked a little bit uncomfortable and I asked her how her sales were progressing. She said that she was using the products she had ordered and sold three toothpastes to her colleagues. She was pleased that people were interested, however no one on social media was asking about the products.

Sarah asked Nina if she had mentioned the business to her family and Nina said that she in fact wanted to ask us about it, as her dad had warned her that this sounded like a Pyramid Scheme. Sarah scoffed at this and said this was typical of family, doubting the business and trying to warn us off it. Nina immediately came to her dad's defence and said that he was only looking out for her best interests. Sarah said that if her family really loved her, they would support her no matter what. I could feel the atmosphere becoming a little awkward and asked Nina if she thought she would be continuing to buying the products and promote them. At this point, Nina was no longer looking at Sarah and had turned her body towards me. She said she was of course happy to earn a little bit of extra pocket money from this, simply selling the products, but didn't want to build teams or recruit. Nina said that working full time in the nail salon didn't give her enough time to dedicate to another business. She worked long hours and when she got home, she simply wanted to relax. Sarah had lost interest at this stage and got up to leave, which I thought was a bit rude. Nina looked perplex at our abrupt departure and I told her I would message her in a few days' time to ask how she was doing with her sales and if she needed any help, she simply needed to reach out.

As Sarah marched out, I quietly apologised to Nina, she was fine and said that her boyfriend and dad had heard of these types of businesses and had told her they didn't think it was a good idea. Nina didn't see the harm in selling the products, but that was as far as she wanted to take it. She didn't want to attend the events, meetings or group Zoom calls. We said goodbye and I met Sarah back downstairs by her car. She didn't look happy and told me that this meeting had been a complete waste of time. I was shocked by her attitude, what had happened to the "positive thinking' and friendly, welcoming nature we were told to apply to TrueVisage recruits?

Sarah told me that she was annoyed by Nina's family disregarding the TrueVisage business without knowing the facts. She said that she could tell Nina wasn't serious about the business and didn't want me to waste my time on her. I felt like Sarah was hiding something and felt that she was perhaps a little stressed out. During the drive home, I asked her what was the matter as the outburst in the café was totally unlike her. She slumped a little in her seat and said she had been feeling under pressure by Chloe with regards to sales and recruitment. Sarah's Upline had apparently introduced new weekly targets within her team and now wanted Sarah to hit a certain number of new recruits and sales.

I was shocked at this, I mean, Sarah was her own boss, she didn't work for Chloe. Sarah now had to participate in weekly Zoom calls with Chloe as well as out weekly group calls. She also needed to hit her target. Why was Sarah allowing herself to be bullied and pressured by this woman? Chloe also insisted that her team join her on a two week long meditation course, which would be held at 6am each morning. The course was designed to bring success to your life and in turn, your business. I was asked by Sarah if I wanted to join the Meditation course, to which I declined. I had a weird feeling about Chloe and wasn't keen on the idea of becoming part of her "team". I was happy to branch out on my own and be independent. I don't think Sarah liked this; however, she knew I wasn't going to be influenced by Chloe and I guess she resented my "freedom".

Sarah asked me if I had booked my ticket for the TrueVisage event in Milton Keynes which was coming up, another £40 I couldn't afford. Chloe was hosting along with another top earner, Diane. I really didn't want to go as Mike (Mr Bully from the January Success Summit) was also going to be there, however it was drilled into us that if we were wanted to be successful and if we were serious about our businesses, we needed to attend all of the events. I said that of course I would go and that James had offered to drive us there.

When I got home, I told James about our meeting with Nina and he said Sarah shouldn't have pressured Nina into TrueVisage. Some people will be happy to be part of it, and others won't – it's not for everyone. I confirmed that he was still willing to drive us to Milton Keynes for the mini event and he said yes. I also wanted to begin planning my Product Launch and started to look into possible venues in London. I wanted to make it as easy as possible for people to come to the launch and knew that travelling to Hertfordshire would put some people off. I made a list of venues in Islington, which is where most of my friends and family live. The only issues were that hiring out a venue or a space would be quite expensive. I looked into church halls; however, this wasn't the right "look" for Linda Beauty. All of the other, more glamourous options would end up costing me over a thousand pounds to hire. Money which I wasn't prepared to spend.

In the end, and after two trips into London to look at potential venues, I decided that I would simply host at home. It would be cosy and informal and would save me a considerably amount of money, which Sarah pointed out, I could spend on products for the showcase. I set the date which would be a Saturday afternoon and made a list of a few products which I would order so that people could try them out. Sarah offered to loan me some of her products also. I wanted to put on a really good showcase in order to look professional and hopefully, convince my friends and family that this was a serious business. I placed my product order and sent a good vibe prayer up to the Universe that this product showcase would hopefully lead to sales and sign-ups.

Chapter 28

Super Saturday had arrived – this was another name allocated to TrueVisage Saturday Events. As Sarah and I were part of the set-up team, we headed off early in order to get to Milton Keynes for 10am. I felt bad that James was driving us there, even though he had offered, he would need to kill time on the day and I wasn't sure how long the meeting was set to last for. When we arrived, James dropped us off and told us to call him once we were finishing up, he decided to simply drive back home and come back to pick us up again.

Sarah and I made our way in doors and I immediately noticed some of the girls from our St Albans group in the lobby. We grabbed a quick coffee and waited for the conference to open. Chloe and Diane were milling around in the lobby, greeting people and Sarah looked nervous. The hold Chloe had over her was strange. I only thing I knew about Chloe was that she and Sarah had gone to the same school together, and that Chloe had friended Sarah on Facebook a few years ago and that's how she was introduced to TrueVisage.

Chloe appeared and asked Sarah and I to follow her upstairs in order to help with the room set up. We were basically there to set up the chairs into rows and move tables from the store room to the front of the meeting room. There was also a screen and projector set up, thankfully we didn't need to do this. As Sarah and I were arranging the furniture, a group of women entered the room and immediately took over, bustling about and setting out products onto the table – I stopped what I was doing and sat down to watch. These girls were from the glam squad and were part of Mike's entourage. He burst through the doors, larger than life and asked everyone how they were and if they were ready to "smash this business today!" He seemed so false and over the top. He started talking to one of the girls, bragging about how he had just now recruited the man serving him in Costa

116

Coffee – "it's that easy!" he bellowed - "I am running my business, while waiting for my Macha Latte!"

It was time for the event to start and the room began to fill up. There were approximately 150 of us in the room, lots of fresh faces eager to find out more about this amazing business opportunity, a way to change your life for the better so you could start to live your best life. All invited by trusted friends and family members. Mike took the stage and welcomed every in the exact same way as we had been welcomed back in January – it felt like a life time ago. It was the same format – we were warmly welcomed and told that because we were here, we had chosen to become a success and change our lives. Those who were not here, were going to be stuck in a boring life, working in a boring job, making money for someone else.

Mike told us his "story". Another rags to riches tale about how he was working long hours in an office job, he hardly spent time with his wife and kids and was "tired of being tired". He was introduced to this business opportunity by an online friend. He declined for months, however whenever he was on Facebook, he noticed on his friend's page that he was posting pictures of himself living this amazing life, surrounded by nice cars, nice clothes and seemed to always be off on luxury holidays. Eventually, Mike got in touch and asked him about the business opportunity and that he wanted to know more. "This was the best thing I have ever done" Mike said. As I looked around the room, I saw the same look in everyone's eyes that were in mine back the first meeting I had attended with Sarah in St Albans.

Everyone was in awe that a normal person just like them, had taken advantage of this business opportunity and had turned their life around. It didn't take Mike long to switch into his Mr Bully character and began calling people out about their body language, exactly as he had done back in January. Anyone with arms crossed were picked on as being standoff-ish and disinterested. He then asked everyone in the room to leave if they were not taking this seriously.

No one left of course, and he then applauded us all for our dedication. It was like some really weird mind game.

Mike then proceeded to run through the business model, it felt like I had heard it a million times. He went on and on about how such a simple plan could make you so much money, however it was up to us to make it a success using the power of positive thinking and never giving up. We were the failures if we gave up on the business, as the business would never give up on us. We needed to be patient and to trust in TrueVisage and to trust in the process. We needed to attend all meetings, events and Success Summit. We were also encouraged to spread the word as much as possible about TrueVisage, everyone could be approached – shop workers, waitresses, hairdressers. The world was your oyster. After Mike had finished, he then went on to introduce another top earner of TrueVisage, Diane – who was actually a friend of Anna's the speaker at the St Albans meeting I first went to.

I can only describe Diane as a woman possessed by TrueVisage. She took the business to another level and was hungry to succeed that it was almost oozing out of her pores. Whenever she spoke, her eyes widened to the point at which I thought her eyeballs were going to pop out of her head. I honestly believed that if you uttered a single word against TrueVisage, she would unleash hell onto you. Diana took the stage and pretty much-repeated everything Mike had said about the business and said that the only way she such a success is because she dedicates all her time to it. She sets herself targets and doesn't stop until she reaches them. She had sign up's all over the world and regards herself as an "International Entrepreneur".

It's funny when I look back it just didn't add up. All of these so called TrueVisage Success stories, bragged about how much money they were making yet shopped in budget high street shops, not that there is anything wrong with this of course. However, casting my mind back to that meeting, Diane didn't come across as someone earning five figure sums by working her TrueVisage business. Her shoes were plastic, scuffed and desperately needed new heels. Her wool dress was synthetic, bobbled and worn. Her handbag was tatty and the handle looked threadbare. Her nails were chipped and her hair extensions had seen better days. I'm not saying you need to be dripping in diamonds and be dressed in designer brands from top to toe, however when you see truly successful people, people who have money, they tend to look sharp, polished and well groomed. Diane's real-life appearance was very different to the photo's she uploaded to Instagram.

The only person who looked like a true success was the American Motivational Speaker who had given the talk at the January Success Summit. I still believe to this day that he was a business man, paid to talk at events by TrueVisage. He may have an investment in the business; however, he is not a TrueVisage representative selling beauty products, that's for sure! On and on the meeting went and it was the same information I had heard at all of the other meetings and events I had attended. These were designed to pump the TrueVisage vision into you on a regular basis. I was frankly bored of hearing it all. It was never anything new – we were there to make up numbers and to show any new recruits that the room was full of TrueVisage representatives living their best life and dedicated to the cause.

Sarah was always full of enthusiasm. She hung on every word and looked up to the other girls and Mike. Whilst Diane droned on and on about how we could make our business a success my mind wondered.…I kept *wanting* to believe in TrueVisage and didn't want to throw in the towel, as every day that went by all I could think was, one more day, one more day and I'll get a big sale or a sign up. The sign up's I had were pointless, as none of them wanted to start their own TrueVisage business. I was throwing money away on products which in truth I hated using and thought were rubbish. I had made new TrueVisage friends who now followed me on Instagram and Facebook and I felt like I was part of a small, close knit family all geared around TrueVisage and its principles of positivity and success. I hadn't alienated my old friends or family, however at this stage I felt I was drifting further and further away from them as none of them supported me and I was encouraged to ditch them by TrueVisage as they were seen as a negative influence. I was constantly being told that they didn't care about me or my business.

When I had spoken to my TrueVisage group on WhatsApp, I was told that I should give my non-TrueVisage friends and family another chance and that my Product Showcase would be the final chance for them to prove that they were going to support me by attending and by purchasing products. Anyone who doesn't attend, doesn't truly care and are blatantly jealous of me wanting to make something of myself. I snapped out of my day dream just as Diane was wrapping up her talk. Mike took the stage and said he was going to photograph the room to post on his social media. He rudely asked three of the women in the front row to vacate their seats so that Diane, Chloe and Anna could sit in them for his photo. The other women were obviously not glamourous enough for him! Once again, another example of staging a photo to make it look like something else.

I was ready to leave and messaged James to come and pick us up. Sarah was saying her goodbyes and I said I would meet her downstairs in the car park. Before I could escape, she called Chloe over. Chloe was all smiles and made a show of telling me how proud she was of me securing Cathy the Gym Owner as a sign up. She and Sarah were both beaming at me and Chloe said that if I carried on the way I was going; I would be picking up a pin title in no time. Despite her praise, I felt empty inside. It meant nothing and I certainly didn't feel successful. I had been ploughing away at my business for over five months, investing all of my energy and money and had made nothing. I had signed up four people – all of which had only done so in order to save money on extortionately priced products. I hardly felt like Richard Branson. I felt like a fake and a phoney. I also hated the fact that every time I signed someone up, I did so under the pretence that I was some major success story, duping people in process. Five months is nothing in business terms, I know this, but it honestly felt like a lifetime in terms of how much time I constantly spent on TrueVisage and when you constantly hear stories of people smashing four to five figures in two to three months, it was hard not to feel like a failure.

I said my goodbye to Chloe, told Sarah I would meet her in the car downstairs and walked out of the room. I had a huge order of products ready for my Product Showcase, I had a handful of people coming to my home event and that small shoot of doubt growing in the pit of my stomach could no longer be squash with positive thinking – it was now a full-on oak tree in bloom.

Chapter 29

Two days before my Product Showcase party was due to take place, I received a text message from one of my Non-TrueVisage friends. This particular friend I had known since I was three years old and we were and still are, really close. I had met up for her for lunch when I was first starting out with TrueVisage and when I told her that I was setting up my very own business, partnered with a Multi-Level-Marketing company, she too, just like many others warned me to be careful, as it sounded very much like a pyramid scheme. I was surprised to hear that years ago she too had dabbled in Multi-Level-Marketing, with an herbal company years ago, however she explained that she had spent a small fortune, attended endless meetings and make a miniscule amount of money back. She invested over a year of her time and money and in the end, decided to quit. At the time of her explaining all of this to me, I secretly thought that she had been the problem, that she had quit, given up on her dreams of success and that this would not be the road I would follow. I would prove that I could make my business a success – just as TrueVisage had coached me.

I clicked on her text message and felt a tingle of dread begin to form in the pit of my stomach. She wrote that there was a documentary airing on television on the day of my Product Showcase which was about Multi-Level-Marketing companies and how they scam people, she went on to write that TrueVisage were being featured on the documentary and she suggested that perhaps I watch it, just in case they say anything negative about them. This was the first I had heard about this. My Product Showcase was just two days away and I couldn't believe what I was reading. Just as I was about to put my phone down, another text came through, from another friend, warning me about the same documentary.

I decided to call Sarah, as surely, she would know about this? Surely the TrueVisage Head Office would know about this? Why hadn't we been notified? I called Sarah and got no answer. I sent her a text message asking her if she knew about the documentary and what was it about exactly, why were they investigating TrueVisage as a scam? I didn't have to wait long for her response. It was very nonchalant, explaining that yes, she knew about the documentary and that the reason why Head Office hadn't mentioned it was because they were against any of us watching it. She told me to wait, as she was about to send a WhatsApp message out to the group, sent from one of the top Uplines.

I remember I was in my kitchen, leaning up against the counter, waiting for the message to come through. I was shocked and didn't know what to make of what I had just read. My phone pinged and I quickly opened up the message. We were told to not watch the documentary and to boycott the programme. It was negative energy and everything in the documentary was false. Yes, the journalist had secretly filmed one of the TrueVisage meetings, however what was said during the meetings was taken out of context. The documentary was focusing on three different companies, one of which was TrueVisage, however Head Office were seeking legal advice and that under no circumstances should be watch the programme. It was blown over as negative, the people making the documentary were jealous and that the information in it was basically false.

I didn't feel that the explanation was good enough. The fact that a well know, respectable television channel was broadcasting a documentary claiming that TrueVisage was a scam really alarmed me. I was confused and very concerned. My phone pinged into life, all three WhatsApp groups were in overdrive as everyone wrote that they were not going to watch the documentary, that they were going to ignore it and that everyone involved were just haters. We were also lightly warmed that if we did watch it, we were basically betraying TrueVisage and that we didn't take the business seriously. My world was spinning and I needed to sit down. I had turned my phone onto silent mode as I didn't want to read anymore. My Non-TrueVisage friends had both messaged me asking me if I was okay, as I had not replied. I typed back that all was well and that the documentary was nothing serious. Head Office had known about it ages ago and didn't think it was serious enough that they needed to notify us.

The truth was that I didn't want to lose face with my friends and admit how worried I was. Even after reading the messages and knowing about the documentary I was still too brainwashed to believe that TrueVisage could be wrong and that it could be a scam. I still wanted to believe I could be a success even with the niggling doubt building up inside of me. I had my Product Showcase coming up in two days and I wanted to prove how amazing the TrueVisage and my business was to everyone.

Chapter 30

It was the day of my Product Showcase and nothing more had been mentioned about the documentary, it was as if we hadn't heard about it. I woke up early and went downstairs in order to prepare the dining room table which would be where I would lay out all of the products. I had purchased various props and stands in order to decorate the table. I wanted it to look professional and inviting. The products on their own would look rubbish, therefore I needed the added an array of props, stands and decorations to disguise the fact that the products weren't that great.

I wasn't looking forward to the day at all. Despite sending out invites, text messages and emails to my friends, family and old colleagues, only my mum, aunt, cousin, sister, sister-in-law and niece were coming. Sarah and her mum, Julia would also be there of course and I had managed to get my Travel Agent Contact from my Local Network Marketing Meeting to come along, as well as my gardener's wife. That was it, ten people. I didn't want to open my home to strangers, therefore didn't announce the party to everyone online. I had invested quite a bit of money on the products I was showcasing in order to have a good selection of skincare and makeup to sell. None of my friends were interested in coming, as they knew that this was a blatant sales pitch. I felt like a child playing shop and was so glad that I hadn't spent a fortune in hiring out a private venue space in London, that would have been a disaster!

I had spoken to James about the documentary and he said we should definitely watch it. I was still in two minds. I wanted to watch it; however, I was scared of what I was going to see and hear. Sarah was of course adamant that she wasn't going to watch it and as far as she was aware, I wasn't going to either. I put the thought out of my mind and finished off setting up the display. Sarah was the first to arrive at midday with Julia. She was buzzing with excitement and thrilled at how great my set up was. She kept on telling Julia how amazing I was at the business and that I was smashing it. I couldn't help but wonder at what she saw when she looked at me and how my business was going. I wasn't "smashing" it at all! My sign-ups (the four that I had) hadn't ordered anymore products, and I didn't hear from them at all. I had made absolutely no money and pretended to be a success online and to my friends and family. It was as if Sarah as living in some weird reality which was the complete opposite to what was actually going on.

This product showcase was the final push, I needed to sell products today. My worry must have been written over my face as Julia was looking at me with concern and as Sarah excused herself to use the toilet, Julia asked me how I was. Again, not wanting to lose face and moan about my failing business, I pretended that everything was alright and that I was really looking forward to the Spain Success Trip the following month. Julia was pleased I was going to be there with Sarah and as Sarah re-appeared, she squeezed my arm and told me she couldn't wait. The trip was apparently, going to change my life!

The doorbell rang, it was my sister-in-law and niece who made their way through to the conservatory, where I had laid out nibbles and refreshments. They didn't so much as glance at my products on display, which left me deflated. My mum and aunt were next to arrive. They both stopped to look at the table which I had painstakingly prepared, however upon noticing the price tags, my aunt exclaimed at how expensive the products were. At this stage, I felt like tipping the table over and leaving the house. Everyone was sat in the conservatory as if it was just a family get together – the products didn't come into the equation! I tried not to let their lack of interest get to me, I picked up a couple of product brochures and casually dropped them into the small table in front of everyone. No one batted an eyelid. It was becoming clear that they were not here for the products, they had come to show support yes, but not actually buy. Again, the feeling of child playing shop sprang to mind. I was so disappointed. Sarah got Julia up and said she would give her a makeover, at this stage, the doorbell rang again and my sister and cousin arrived. My heart literally burst with love when they bee lined straight for the table and immediately began trying the products. They both seemed genuinely interested and as I had purchased eight different shades of lip gloss, my cousin was keen to try them all. Things were looking up and when my Travel Agent Contact and Gardener's wife showed up, they too were keen to check out the products.

I was pouring wine and handing our nibbles keen to keep the positive atmosphere going. I was hopeful that I would sell some products. After all of the planning and stock purchased, I sold one body lotion. I made £6. By 4pm everyone had left except Sarah who offered to help me tidy up. I had kept a smile plastered on my face throughout the whole of the afternoon but what I really wanted to do was cry and rant angrily about how no one cared about my business, and that my family and "so called" friends didn't want to support me. I had become angry, bitter and resentful. That day, surrounded by TrueVisage products, I felt like I had f**ked up big time. I had yet to watch the documentary.

Chapter 31

Sarah and I tidied up in silence, I think she could sense something was wrong. She asked if I was okay and I made up the excuse that I was tried, feeling run down and all of the excitement of the Product Launch as caught up with me. I told her she was okay to leave, that I could finish up on my own. James had just got back, having made himself scarce for the afternoon and had settled himself down on the couch. Just as Sarah was putting her coat on, he asked me if I wanted to watch the documentary. I froze on my way into the living room, Sarah stopped buttoning up her coat and looked at me. James, was completely oblivious to the atmosphere and proceeded to load the programme onto the screen. I looked at Sarah and told her I was going to watch it. In truth, I was curious. I wanted to know what was going to be said about TrueVisage. I could see the panic in Sarah's face, with a strained smile set on her face, she took off her coat and said that we may as well watch it together.

The truth was, I realise now, was that she wanted to be there to monitor my reaction and to contradict anything negative that was said. She practically talked throughout the whole thing. The documentary started and I watch in horror as the truth about TrueVisage unfolded before my eyes. For 60 minutes, I felt like I was being punched over and over again in my stomach. I felt like I had been in a coma and was finally walking up. Like a fog was being lifted from my brain. All of the light that had gone out of me over the last five months, was finally shining.

I watched as the journalist picked apart the TrueVisage business model, as she interviewed other poor women who had been duped and brainwashed just like me, just like Sarah! How they had lost hundreds, some thousands of pounds buying the products which they could not sell. I watched as the journalist secretly filmed Anna, the £19,000 earner who I first saw in St Albans bragging about duping people into the businesses. I watched as at the meeting one of the TrueVisage top Uplines told everyone to cut their friends and family out of their lives. I watched as experts and phycologists explained the pitfalls of Multi-Level-Marketing companies and how they use Cult Like Tactics to trap people and brainwash them. I watched as they explained that only a small and I mean miniscule amount of people make money with MLM companies.

I saw the faces of people I had met; I saw the same video promoting the Spain Success Summit Trip played, all tools to get people to part with their cash. I watch as the journalist explained that the majority of these Multi-Level-Marketing companies are founded in the World capital of MLM's which is Utah, in the USA where they employ the same cult like recruitment tactics that many religious groups do, such as knocking on doors, and approaching people in public places, it all had a very extremist religious feel to it. At most of the events, being part of the MLM was seen as being "part of global mission" just like religious cults.

I watched as the journalist interviewed Network Marketing Groups and Mother and Toddler Groups who refused to have anyone associated with MLM companies as part of their groups as they knew that they were scams. I watched as the journalist secretly filmed at the Success Summit of another MLM beauty company, which used the exact same format as TrueVisage. All designed to make you fall for the lies. I watched, I watched, I watched the nightmare unfold and with every blink of my eyes I flashed back over the last five months and how it all now fell into place. I had been conned, lied to and had been made to look a fool.

Sarah gave a running commentary throughout the whole documentary. She blasted it as being totally false and made up. She was outraged at how they had managed to secretly film the meetings and events and even attached the poor women being filmed, shouting at the television that the journalist had chosen the ugliest women – no wonder their beauty businesses had failed! I couldn't hear Sarah anymore over the blood rushing around my ears. I wanted her out of my house and I wanted to be left alone. My brain had been assaulted and I couldn't take any more in. The documentary had finished and James looked at me, concern flooded his face, he got up and politely asked Sarah to leave, explaining that today had been "eventful" and that we needed to prepare dinner and relax for the evening. I remember Sarah being completely oblivious to everything, she bounced out the house, telling me that she would call me tomorrow, I remember hearing something about running a stall with her at Hatfield Council the following week.

As James closed the front door behind Sarah, I got up from the sofa in a zombie like state and went upstairs. I had a throbbing head ache and wanted to be alone. James sensing my mood, told me he was downstairs if I needed him and that he would sort dinner out. The last thing I wanted to do was eat. I got into bed, closed my eyes and tried to erase the utter feeling of humiliation I felt in every cell in my body.

Chapter 32

I woke the next day feeling awful. It was as if my body and mind were breaking down and all I wanted to do was exorcise TrueVisage out of my life. I felt like I was coming down with a rotten cold and was showing all of the symptoms. After I showered, I plopped myself down on the sofa, curled up into a ball and put my mobile phone onto silent mode. I didn't want to hear from anyone, friends, family, TrueVisage. I had had enough. I wanted out and I was going to start now.

I opened up my Instagram account and immediately began to delete all of the TrueVisage related posts I had uploaded onto my page. I deleted the positivity posts, the videos, "my Story" post, everything. I unfollowed all of the other TrueVisage representatives except for Sarah. I logged into my Linda Beauty Facebook account and deleted it. I hated having a Facebook page and deleting the account made me feel like I had lifted a weight off of my shoulders.

I then messaged my Downlines, Clara first – I felt awful having to write to her explaining that the TrueVisage was a scam, that I had been duped and in turn, had duped her. I apologised. I told her that if she wanted to cancel her TrueVisage account, she would need to contact them directly. As I was going to deactivate mine in the coming days, any commission would automatically pass onto Sarah. I told Clara that I of course still wanted to remain friends, however I understood if she didn't and I of course, wouldn't blame her.

I then messaged my Travel Agent Friend and Nina, explaining to both of them my decision and why I was quitting. I was honest and open with them both. I knew that they were not planning on starting their own beauty business, and I hadn't heard from them since we last spoke, however I wanted to give them an explanation all the same.

Deleting my posts, refreshing my Instagram account and cutting off TrueVisage contacts immediately made me feel better. I was still reeling from the documentary, I felt betrayed, used and foolish, however I took on some of what I had learned regarding positivity (the true and natural way) and having a positive mindset and this is what kept me going. Now and then, James asked if I was okay. I told him how I was feeling. He put his arms around me and told me that he was pleased I had come to the decision to stop my partnership with TrueVisage. James never really agreed with it, however he thought it was making me happy and saw how determined I was and didn't want to go against it. He knew that if he objected, it would drive a wedge between us. His plan was to ride it out, until I saw sense and he knew that eventually I would. He was just glad it was now, only after a few months and not a year or two down the line.

I still had to break the news to Sarah and I had to think about how I was going to deal with Cathy, the gym owner and what I was going to do about the Spain Success Summit that was coming up in two weeks' time. Cathy wasn't really a problem; I would contact her on Monday morning and explain everything. The Success Summit was a different matter altogether, as I had already paid for the ticket, the flight and I had reserved the hotel. I knew this was going to be hard for Sarah to hear and despite the fact that she had dragged me into all of this, I felt no bad feelings towards her. It's weird really, I genuinely didn't feel angry towards her rather, I felt sorry for her. She had been brainwashed by TrueVisage for almost *five* years. It was going to be a lot harder for her to leave. I truly believed that after seeing the documentary that Sarah was going to be exactly like me, that she would want to leave, however just as I was settling down to enjoy the rest of the weekend with James, I saw a text from her on my phone.

Sarah was reminding me that on Wednesday we were running a stall at Hatfield Council. She had secured a table in the canteen area months ago and I had promised her we would run it together. I remember her saying it had been really hard to secure it and that being there all day meant a constant flow of people to and from the canteen area, up to 400 people. I really didn't want to do it, however it dawned on me that I was now left with TrueVisage stock I needed to get rid of. I couldn't bear the thought of pretending for another three days, however I needed to try and claw back as much money as I could. I resigned myself to the fact that I would need to prolong telling Sarah that I was quitting the business until Thursday.

I messaged back, telling Sarah that I had a bad cold and that hopefully, I would be well by Wednesday and that I would of course, help her with the stall. I said that over the next couple of days I would be "out of action" trying to recover from my cold. I didn't want to be contacted by anyone and I hope she took the hint. She wished me well and said she would see me at her place on Wednesday morning at 10am. I switched my phone off, and snuggled down onto the sofa and relaxed in the knowledge that I had three more days left and then I would be free of TrueVisage world and its lies.

Chapter 33

The following day, James went to work and I watched the documentary again. I needed to hear all of the information once more, without Sarah prattling off in the background. As I watched, I couldn't help but laugh at my stupidity and the way that I had fallen for the cult tactics and brainwashing. How could I have been so blind? Why had I fallen for all of the bullsh*t? I ran a search on the television and found two other documentaries which also focused on cult like tactics used in Multi-Level-Marketing companies. I was shocked at how many people, from all walks of life fall victim to them. I was astonished at how big the companies were and that they operated all over the world. The thing that shocked me the most was that these companies and their practices were not being regulated, as technically they were not breaking any laws.

Over the next two days I research online and read articles about TrueVisage, digging deeper and deeper and what I found was shocking. Law suits against the company in other countries which claimed it was running an illegal pyramid scheme, law suits against the founders. Countless people posting anonymous, negative reviews. There was already a huge backlash on social media following the documentary aimed at the journalist. It seemed that speaking up against these companies was not a good idea.

I logged into my TrueVisage account and emailed Head Office with regards to sending back my stock and claiming a refund. I was told that I could of course send items back, however they had to be unopened and of course, not used. There was a slight problem with this, in that I had opened the product boxes in order to showcase my products at my Products Launch. The actually products however were brand new, only some had been used. I needed to think about how to get around this as there was no way I was willing to lose all of the money I had spent.

I began sorting out the products I would take to the Hatfield Council stall on Wednesday, hoping that I could shift the lot. I was tired of seeing the items in my home and wanted to be rid of it all. Sarah had messaged me on Tuesday saying that the last time she ran the stall she had sold loads of products and had managed to secure several new sign-ups, however I read her message not believing a single word as everything she had said to me over the last five months had been a lie, I couldn't really believe anything she said to me now and it dawned on me that carrying on a friendship with her now was going to be difficult. I guess as long as she didn't speak about TrueVisage, we would be okay. I was wrong, and the next few days would prove that TrueVisage didn't just ruin your trust and finances, it ruined relationships too.

Chapter 34

My last day as a TrueVisage phoney had arrived and the only thing I was looking forward to was selling as much of my product stock as possible. I drove to Sarah's house and parked up outside, knowing that I would have to pretend to be enthusiastic about the day. I was still feeling ill and hoped that I could blame my cold for my lack of interested in all things TrueVisage related. Sarah came out of the house, and I climbed out of my car with my bag full of products and props and pop them inside the boot of her car.

I got into the passenger's seat and we greeted each other, call me paranoid but I sensed she knew my true feelings. She wasn't as warm in her greeting towards me and as she drove to the Hatfield Council Offices she spoke about the documentary and how everyone within the TrueVisage community were livid about it. No one believed it and we were being told to completely disregard the programme. Sarah told me that she would always be true to TrueVisage and that nothing or nobody would convince her otherwise. TrueVisage was her life and she would work towards making her business a success and getting to the top of the pin title ladder.

I think her talk in the car was geared towards me. I knew she had been monitoring my Instagram page and had seen all of the changes I had been making over the last few days. She hadn't questioned me yet, however I felt it wouldn't be long before she asked me what was going on. Her lecture in the car was her way of getting me back on side and getting me motivated again.

We arrived at the Council Offices and Sarah parked up by the back doors which lead to a staff entrance. She asked me to wait in the car while she spoke with the security team in order to obtain our guest passes for the day. Still feeling like death warmed up, I took two paracetamol and hoped that the day would pass quickly. Once inside, we were showed to the canteen by the building manager. We had been allocated space by the entrance to the canteen and there was a long trestle table and two chairs that we could use. It was already 11:30am and we needed to set up quickly if were we going to be ready for the main lunchtime rush.

We both unpacked the products and props, laying a large white table cloth across the table and hastily placing palm tree leave mats out which we would display our product on. We virtually halved the table and I arranged my items as best as I could, aware that the Council Office lunch break would be commencing soon. Whilst we prepared, Sarah rattled on about how last year she had sold loads and made good money. She also said that I should make a note of the names and email addresses of anyone interested in the products so that I could follow up with them in the days to come and try to recruit them. In my mind of course, I was telling Sarah to get lost. There was no way I was going to recruit anyone into this scam.

We were finally ready, and our TrueVisage stall was open. I felt so amateur and I resented being there, however I wanted to try to make the most of it and plastered a smile on my face despite that fact that my nose was running like a tap and my throat was sore. It was as if my body was rejecting all things TrueVisage and a rotten cold was its way of doing it. I plopped myself down on one of the seats and thankfully Sarah offered to buy me a cup of tea, which I gracefully accepted, it was one of the rare occasions she offered to pay for anything when we were together.

A slow trickle of people began making their way into the canteen. It was a natural reaction as you walked into the room, to glance over to our area as it was right by the entrance, however most of the people simply carried on walking. A few came over to have a quick look, noticed the price tags and carried on walking. It was going to be a long afternoon. Sarah said that this was common, and that sales tended to happen after people had eaten their lunch. I wanted to tell her to stop lying, I wanted to tell her to just stop talking. I wanted to tell her that I didn't believe the crap coming out of her mouth, instead, I just smiled and said that I was sure sales would pick up.

I had lost my appetite and Sarah popped over to the sandwich cart to pick up some lunch. I swallowed another two paracetamol and willed myself to carry on sitting there like some sad case. Two women made their way over and began to look at products, one of them commented on the price, saying that it was way more than she would normally spend and that she had never heard of TrueVisage – in my mind I was agreeing with her. Sarah practically bounced over to the table, threw her sandwich at me and began to give two women a brief history of the company. This was when one of the women said "I won't be buying; did you see the Documentary on Saturday? This was one of the companies on it, it's a scam". At this point I wanted the floor to open and swallow me up. The look the two women gave us as they left was awful, as if Sarah and I had the plague.

I just stared at the floor; however, Sarah was fuming. She began ranting on about how the two women were just jealous and didn't know what they were talking about. How dare they judge us. How dare they! Who were they to tell us that this amazing company was a scam? Sarah said she was going to ignore them and not let their negative comments affect her – although clearly, they already had.

I busied myself rearranging products. The afternoon was dragging and by some miracle, Sarah managed to sell a body lotion. This was to the same receptionist she had sold to last year, or as Sarah called her "a loyal customer". By 3pm, I was ready to leave and I convinced Sarah that we should pack up as lunch time was well and truly over and I hadn't sold anything. In a way, I wasn't at all surprised, despite Sarah harping on that we would make a killing in sales. This was yet another exaggeration from her.

I was silent on the drive back to Sarah's house. I used my sore throat as an excuse to say little and let Sarah rattled on about the Spain Success Trip and how much she was looking forward to it. This was the time for me to tell her that I was done with TrueVisage, however I didn't have the strength to have it out with Sarah in the car. We arrived at her place, where upon I exchange my place from her car to mine, just before I said goodbye, Sarah reminded me of the St Albans meeting that evening. It had completely slipped my mind. I told Sarah I wasn't going to go, as I was too ill to attended and didn't really wanted to spread my cold around the room.

She agreed, and offered instead to send me a Zoom link so that I could attended from home as she would be bringing her laptop and could connect me to the meeting. I pretended to pleased she was being so thoughtful – one last pointless meeting for me to attend before being free of TrueVisage for good.

Chapter 35

Once home, I changed into some comfortable loungewear, took another dose of cold remedy and settled down onto the sofa for some much-needed rest. I told James about my day once he was home from work and he congratulated me on getting through it and on the fact that come tomorrow, I would free of TrueVisage once and for all. It's funny when I look back that I didn't feel myself truly free until I had told Sarah. It was as if I needed to cut some sort of inviable umbilical cord with her. She was the one who introduced me; therefore, I would only be free once I told her I wasn't going to be part of it any longer.

Our friendship had been so intense over the past five months, we practically saw and/or spoke to each other every day. We practically lived in each other's pockets and here I was, one day away from telling her this was all over. I hoped we could salvage a small part of our friendship, however I knew deep down that that was going to be impossible as the message TrueVisage drove into us all was that anyone against TrueVisage was a negative entity and that they were dream stealers, determined to dragged you away from your TrueVisage dreams of success. As soon as I stopped, I knew our friendship would too. I would be dead wood, Sarah would no longer earn money from my purchases or sales, therefore why bother to be my friend.

At 6:55pm, Sarah texted me my Zoom log in details so that I could join in on the St Albans meeting. She had obviously briefed all of the usually attendees and senior representatives of my "lack of motivation', as soon as I logged in and came into view on her screen, everyone greeted me in an over exaggerated way, all wishing me well and that I was sorely missed. I'm surprised I wasn't asked for my £10 contribution. Behind all the false smiles that never reached the eyes, it was all about business and bleeding people dry. The meeting progressed in the same old way. The PowerPoint Presentation of the business model, the slides showing us all how TrueVisage were advised in all of the top magazines, I always noticed how none of them were British publications, only Chinese or Filipino magazines I didn't recognise. The two hosts, the husband and wife duo gave us the same rags to riches story about how they both quite their jobs to build their TrueVisage business full time - yet another lie, Sarah told me only a couple of weeks ago that the wife was still working part time and the husband was still in full time employment. As Sarah and I became closer she felt she could divulge a few "trade secrets" to me thinking I would relish being included in the duping of people, it actually had the reverse effect and I only ended up hating TrueVisage more.

She once told me that all of the top earners had access to a photo bank of pictures they used on social media. These pictures were the ones I would saw on other people's social media in the beginning, the huge boxes of products "supposedly" being distributed to clients. These boxes were in fact product boxes which were empty, made to look like full boxes of products that were being sent out to clients. All of the lies about inboxes being full of customer messages, were just tricks used to make people think you were a high-flying business owner. I was so naïve that I thought it was real. All of the people who told us they were working the TrueVisage business, were in fact paid speakers. Sarah thought she could tell me this and I would be somehow impressed, when in actual fact I was disgusted by the deceit.

Once the presentation was over, the husband and wife both took the stage and decided to enlighten us with more tips on how we could work our businesses. We were told that we needed to use social media to "fish" for potential clients - I had heard this a million times before, however the next tip was new. We needed to seek out anyone having problems with debt, say difficulties paying off their credit cards and introduce them to this business as a way of them clearing their debts. I suddenly became alert and spoke up, I asked the couple what they meant, surely if someone was in debt, they wouldn't have spare cash to spend on buying TrueVisage products to promote online? The wife piped up and said "You'll find that people with debt just can't help spending, at the end of the day, better they get into more debt filling your pocket than someone else's?

I couldn't believe what I was hearing. Was she actually encouraging us to help people spiral into more debt so that we could profit!? I could see and hear the people in the room actually agreeing with her. My moral compass went into overdrive and had I been in the room, I would have got up and left, however I was glued to my laptop screen waiting to hear what other ludicrous "gold nuggets" of advice she was about to dish out. The husband then chimed in that he and his wife had watched an "exclusive" TrueVisage video tutorial, only for certain representative and they were now pleased to pass on the information, as this was another amazing way to boost our incomes.

Every month, we were asked to purchase 50 units of a certain product and we were to tell all of our downlines to do the same, and they tell their Downlines and so on. This month it would be the toothpaste - 50 units at my wholesale discounted price would be a total of £350. We were then targeted to sell all 50 units in that month. We had to look at this as a challenge. All of my Uplines would profit from me and I would profit from my Downlines. I couldn't sell the rubbish I had now, what made them think I would sell 50 toothpastes – were they insane? Of course, the people at the top of the pyramid must have been rubbing their hands in delight at the thought of this. This was the nail in the TrueVisage coffin as far as I was concerned, I messaged Sarah to say I was too ill to continue and that I was login off. I would call her tomorrow morning as I had something important to discuss with her. I switched off my phone, just in case she messaged or called me back. I took a deep breath and felt an utter sense of relief that I had come to me senses and was one more sleep away from ending this farce once and for all.

Chapter 36

I woke the next morning feeling slightly better, however I wasn't looking forward to my chat with Sarah. I got the impression she knew by now that my initial enthusiasm and love towards TrueVisage had well and truly dwindled. All of my Instagram posts relating to TrueVisage and overly exaggerated positivity posts had been deleted and I had closed down my Facebook account. I knew Sarah had been monitoring all of this as she had been in contact with me less and less over the last few days.

I made myself a cup of tea and sat down with my laptop. I was in the middle of deleting my TrueVisage Contact List and some other files, when my phone pinged – it was Sarah, letting me know that she was driving to her mum and Paul's house and that she would call me for a chat once she had parked up outside. I readied myself for the awkward conversation, which was about to take place, at this point my main concern was how to deal with the Spain Success Summit which I had already paid for. I knew Sarah was relying on me to go with her, however now that I was no longer going to be a part of TrueVisage, I didn't see how I could go. I was certainly not going to attend the Summit.

My phone rang, I answered, trying to sound upbeat. Sarah asked how I was feeling and commented on how much better I sounded. I didn't see the point in beating around the bush and came straight out with it. I explained that my TrueVisage business was no longer something I wanted to continue with. I had had time to seriously reflect over the last week and it just wasn't for me. The line went quiet, for a split second I thought Sarah had hung up on me. I asked Sarah if she was still there – no response. I asked again and then came the sniffling sounds…she was crying. Part of me felt awful that I was responsible for making her cry, however another part of me wanted to tell her to get a grip of herself.

In order to overcome the awkwardness, words began tumbling out of my mouth about how this changed nothing and that we could of course still be friends. I didn't blame Sarah, however after watching the documentary I felt it would be stupid and irresponsible of me to continue given the evidence and facts presented. I had researched online after it was aired and there were so many other anti MLM websites, crammed with expert advice and information on how to get out and leave the cult like environment. I read comments on forum after forum from people who had been scammed, just like me – it was awful, surely Sarah agreed?

Sarah did not agree. She thought I was crazy to give up on the business and that I was failing myself and my dreams. She went on and on about how good I was at selling, despite the fact that I had hardly sold a thing and that it was madness of me to give up now. I realised then and there that Sarah was in too deep. Almost five years of brainwashing had done this to her, she believed every single thing TrueVisage represented. She believed their lies and there was no way I would be able to convince her otherwise. She kept pleading with me not to stop and that we made a good team. She wanted me to at least give it till the end of the year, however my mind was made up. This way of life, the lies and duping, the "fake it till you make it" mentality was not for me. I realised then that I had absolutely nothing in common with Sarah or the other women. The only thing that held us together was TrueVisage and dreams of one day, becoming a success.

I had made my final decision and made it clear to Sarah. The next topic to tackle was how I was going to get around not going to the Success Summit. I now broached the subject to which Sarah sent me on a guilt trip. I had promised to go with her, to help her as she wasn't a confident lone traveller. Julia and Paul were expecting me to go, on and on she went. She even suggested I still go to the Summit to which I flatly refused. Sarah was still crying and I admit, despite the fact that she had introduced me to TrueVisage and profited from me buying the products and continued to spout rubbish to me face the whole seven months I had known her, I couldn't help but feel sorry for her. I wanted to be angry and upset, but just felt pity. I had seen the light, yet she was still very much in the dark.

I had one of two choices, completely cancel the trip and no doubt fall out with Sarah and my cousin Paul and Julia, or go to Spain with Sarah and try to work out a plan which would mean I could still get a little holiday out of it without taking part in any TrueVisage events.

I explained the second option to Sarah who was dubious about how we could make it all work. I said I would fly out with her as planned, we would stay in the hotel together, sharing a room as planned, I would even accompany her to the town centre everyday so she didn't have to wander around on her own, as our hotel was just on the outskirts of town (I admit, I was shocked that she was relying on me this much, I mean she was thirty years old, not a child…) I would then kill time throughout the day and eventually meet up with her so we could make our way back to the hotel together in the evening. I felt I was going above and beyond for her, despite the circumstances.

I could almost see Sarah sticking out her bottom lip in the way a petulant child does. She wasn't happy with the deal. I asked her if she would kindly ask around and see if anyone wanted to buy my ticket for the Success Summit. I was willing to sell it at a discounted price. I also asked her if she wanted to buy any of my stock. I knew this was cheeky of me, however Sarah had squeezed a lot out of me over the last few months and I was still willing to keep the peace and go to Spain, the least she could do was help me recoup some money. She said she would ask around and let me know. We agreed it would be sensible for her to pop round to mine so we could have a proper face to face talk and we also needed to run over the Gym Charity Event, which I of course would no longer be attending. Sarah ended out call saying that she would now have to explain her puffy, red eyes to her mum and that she was in shock that I had quit like this. I didn't apologise, I didn't feel that I needed to. The Spain trip would be a little cross I would have to bear; however, I remember ending the call feeling happy that I was finally free.

Chapter 37

Life had suddenly taken on a more relaxed vibe. I was no longer part of the mobile group chats. I was no longer on Facebook and I no longer felt pressured to continuously post about my "life" on Instagram. I had shaken off the cold and was feeling much better, not just in physical health, but in mental health also. I was still reeling over having been scammed and felt a huge sense of embarrassment. Over the last five months I had been portraying someone who was successful, owner of her own business, hell, I even bragged about being an international entrepreneur purely based on the fact that I had spoken to my old Personal Trainer who lived in France and was potentially signing her up. Following TrueVisage guidance made you that ridiculous.

Sarah no longer messaged me – it was as if I had never known her. I was no longer a human cash machine and she had lost interest. No doubt she had spoken to her Upline Chloe, who had immediately told her to cut ties with me. The thing with TrueVisage and the way they brainwash you is that you are never allowed to complain or be negative, in this I mean that you are never supposed to go against the company and perhaps say that business is not going great, you're not making money or that you don't agree with the way TrueVisage does things. If too many people begin saying these things, then people will start to question the company and the business, hence why they drill you with the positive thinking and positive mindset and to get rid of anyone close to you who is a negative influence. I was now viewed as a dangerous entity by Chloe, if I somehow managed to convince Sarah that what I was saying about TrueVisage was true and Sarah quit the business, Chloe would lose her stream of income from Sarah and her Downlines and their Downlines and so on. As far as Chloe was concerned, I was a bug that needed to be squashed and quickly.

I eventually messaged Sarah to ask if she had managed to find someone to buy my Spain Success Summit ticket. Someone had to make the first move in sorting out this mess and it looked like I had to be the grown up. In the past, Sarah would have replied back almost instantly, however now I was hated, therefore I would have to wait for her responses. After several hours, I received a text from her. Sarah had managed to find another TrueVisage representative to buy my ticket, £40 less than what I had paid. I didn't care, I would still get the majority of my money back and would be rid of the ticket. We agreed that Sarah should come to mine, so that she could give me the money and we could discuss the Gym Charity Event coming up on that Friday and plans for Spain. We agreed a meeting at mine the following day.

I wasn't looking forward to Sarah's visit, but we needed to reach some sort of amicable status if we were going to share a hotel room together for four days, in fact the more I thought about it I was now beginning to think separate rooms would be better. I was happy to foot the bill for the extra room and would mention it to Sarah when she arrived. It was a case of me accompanying her for Pauls and Julia's sake, as I knew they would feel better knowing I was with Sarah on the trip. Sarah arrived early, gently knocking on my front door as if she too knew that the conversation ahead wasn't going to be easy. She came into the living room, a slight smile on her face and although I tried to keep the conversation flowing with pleasantries, it was so forced, I was cringing inside.

She sat down on the sofa and I busied myself in the kitchen making tea, asking after her mum and Paul. Once I was sat down, I began by apologising for the way all this had ended up (I still to this day do not know why I felt like I had to say sorry, I guess I was apologising more for the loss of our friendship than anything else). I wanted to sort everything out and hopefully find a way we could both be happy on our trip to Spain. I mentioned having separate rooms in the hotel, to which Sarah's face fell, however I ploughed on, listing the benefits, such as her having more privacy so that she could speak freely with her husband, Max at the end of each day. The last thing she would want was me listening in while she spoke out the TrueVisage Summit. Sarah was silent; however, I could tell that deep down even she had to admit it was for the best. I then repeated my plan about accompanying her into town and waiting for her to finish up in the evening so that we could make our way back to the hotel together, this was she wouldn't be on her own. I thought I was being super gracious despite what had happened, in truth I didn't need to go to Spain now – I was only going as a favour to my cousin Paul. We agreed on my plan, however Sarah tried one last ditch attempt to convince me to attend the summit and go out with the TrueVisage group in the evening, to which I declined. There was no way I was going to submit myself to more TrueVisage Brainwashing and nonsense. I also wasn't going to be the hated, odd one out at evening dinners. I knew all the other women would resent me being there and would try to get me back into the fold. I wasn't going to put myself through it.

We then moved onto discussing the Gym Charity Event. I explained to Sarah that once I cancelled my TrueVisage account, that Cathy would immediately become her direct Downline and I was absolutely fine with this. Sarah once again tried to convince me to keep my account live, as I would still earn money from Cathy, however I just couldn't do it. I no longer wanted anything to with the company and its lies. It would be two faced of me to still earn money from sales by Downlines, it would be a piddly amount anyway and I wasn't interested. As I looked up, Sarah was silently crying again. I asked her why she was crying and once she regained some composure, she said it was because she couldn't believe I was quitting and she couldn't believe that I was throwing away the opportunity to change my life for the better. I replied saying I couldn't believe she thought all this was real and that she couldn't see beyond all of the TrueVisage bullsh*t.

How could she not see it, especially after having watched the documentary – was she that blind? Could she not see that we were all being made fools of? Could she not see that the only TrueVisage customers buying the products were us! We were the ones earning the money for our Uplines because no one else would buy the rubbish we were peddling. Could she not see that we were just representatives and recruiters, not "our own business directors" or "entrepreneurs". All TrueVisage representatives do was lie. They exploited people's weaknesses and make money from it. The message was to "Empower Women" yet we harped on about them caking themselves in rubbish makeup and try to control the way they think and behave.

I could see that my words were falling on deaf ears, Sarah was far too brainwashed to believe me. Chloe and the others had a much tighter hold on her and I needed to accept it. I asked Sarah if she would see if Cathy wanted to buy my Face Lift Device from me for £100. I knew she was thinking of buying another one and thought I would want to save her some money whilst I tried to claw a little back. I asked Sarah also if she wanted any of the products I had and she declined. Apparently, business was slow (again) and she needed all the money she had for Spain. I wasn't surprised. She gave me the ticket money from the woman who was buying my place at the Success Summit and I gave sent her the e-ticket email.

I wished Sarah luck with the Gym Charity Event; she had managed to get one of her other Downlines to accompany her. She left my house telling me she would message if Cathy purchased the Face Lift Devise and we could finalise meeting at the Airport when we were due to fly out at the end of the following week. I closed the door behind me knowing that the Spain trip was going to be hard work, however it was the last hurdle, I was just going to have to get through it. I decided to treat it like a mini holiday, a chance to reset my old self and come back to the UK to job hunt and get my life back in track.

Chapter 38

I waited until the day after the Charity Event to message Sarah to ask if it had gone well and if she had managed to sell my Face Lift Device to Cathy. I received no response from Sarah. I knew she was punishing me in her own way by giving me the silent treatment, however I couldn't help but be annoyed as I was going out of my way to be nice, despite everything that had happened and all the lies Sarah had told me about TrueVisage and her experiences with them. I still saw her as family and was trying my best to keep things civil between us, what with the Spain trip coming up and for the sake of Paul and Julia.

Sarah's behaviour towards me since I quit my dealings with TrueVisage only further cemented my belief that as soon as you cut ties, any relationship that you have with your Uplines dies. Goodness knows what brainwashing nonsense the other women were feeding Sarah about me. Two days after my initial message I received a message from Sarah. She had decided she no longer wanted to stay in the same hotel as me and was now sharing a room with one of the other girls closer to the town centre. She went on to write that she had managed to sell the Face Lift Device to Cathy, however she was going to keep the £100 pounds for herself, as it was only fair seeing as she was no longer staying in the hotel room with me, therefore the £100 was her share of the room payment.

Sarah only needed me to travel with her on the flight there and back and to be on hand just in case she needed me. I couldn't believe what I was reading. I had to read her message back three times, before it all registered. I was fuming. First of all, how dare she take it upon herself to decide to keep money that was rightfully mine, secondly, she had made changes to her accommodation without bothering to consult me and check if I would be penalised with the booking. Thirdly, she assumed that I was going to go to Spain simple to escort her for the flight then be "on hand" and at her beck and call should she need me – thinking I would drop what I was doing and go running. I was absolutely speechless. Not only was she brainwashed, she was also behaving like a spoilt brat.

Over the last few days, I had tried my best to be civil, to look beyond her lies and deceit. I had genuinely wanted to salvage our friendship, knowing full well that we would never be close, however to keep it so that if I was ever visiting Paul and Julia and Sarah happened to be there also, we could at least be civil towards each other. Her text message was the last straw. I was infuriated and messaged back saying that she was a fool of she thought I would still be going to Spain with her. I would rather forfeit the money for the entire booking. There was absolutely no way I would go simply to chaperon her and be at her beck and call. I told her she could keep the money for the Face Lift Device, she obviously needed the cash more than me. I would refund her the money she had already paid me for the flight, instead of flying business class with me, she could rebook herself on Easy Jet or Ryanair (I know this sentence comes across as petty and snobby, however I knew it would annoy her, I was angry and lashing out – I should have risen above it).

I finished my message saying that I had had enough with bending over backwards to try to be nice to her, she didn't deserve my friendship. She was totally brainwashed by TrueVisage and one day she would wake up and realise that peddling beauty products for a company that didn't pay you a salary was a scam; it didn't make her a "Company Director" nor did it make her an "Entrepreneur". She was a sales person, brainwashed into thinking she was. She needed to wake up and quickly. I wanted to end my message being the bigger person, the sensible one, therefore I ended saying that if one day, she decided to wake up and see the light, I would be there for her, as I knew she would need the support. I am not a horrible person and I knew, deep down, that coming away from TrueVisage and the cult tactics they use would be hard and that Sarah would need true friends to help her.

I didn't receive a reply back and I knew this would be the last I would ever hear from Sarah.

I was shaking and needed to sit down. Never in my life have I ever fallen out with anyone. I have always been a calm and relaxed person. I hate confrontations and avoid arguments. James and I have been married for 16 years and have been together for 18 and I can say hand on heart that we have never argued. Yes, of course we have minor disagreements, but we have never argued. It's just not in me, life's too short.

I sat on end of my bed and immediately felt that I needed to call Julia to explain my side of the story before Sarah filled her head with lies about me. I had a feeling in my gut that I needed to warn Julia that Sarah was in trouble with TrueVisage, that she was brainwashed and that if she wasn't going to listen to me, she might listen to her mum, or Paul. I dialled Julia's number; however, I got no response. Within a couple of minutes, she messaged back saying she was out having lunch with her mum and friend and was just heading home – she would call me once she got in.

I knew I didn't have long and that there was a strong chance that Sarah was making her way round to her mum's as I sat there. I messaged Julia saying that Sarah and I had unfortunately fallen out. I had decided to quit TrueVisage as I strongly believed that it was a cult, brainwashing people to sign up to their Pyramid scheme. I tried to warn Sarah, but she didn't want to listen and I believed that she was in too deep. Julia and Paul needed to intervene. I also explained about Spain and that I had tried to be civil and do the right thing, but that Sarah was taking advantage of my good nature. I was sorry it had come to this, however I wanted Julia and Paul to know the truth.

I waited a few minutes and my phone rang, it was Julia, however just as I answered, she hung up. Sarah had gotten to her first. I knew that just as she was about to speak, Sarah must have arrived or that she was calling her. That was it. Sarah was no doubt going to fill their heads with lies about me and my relationship with my cousin and Julia was ruined also.

Chapter 39

It took me a few days to finally calm down. I know it sounds silly to dwell over something like this, however like I said, this sort of thing has never happened to me before and I felt like our argument had been extremely childish. I was also annoyed at myself and I was still trying to get over having been duped, and made a fool of.

I still needed to tie up some lose ends. I had my stock to get rid of and I didn't want to go through the rigmarole of trying to sell it all on eBay or Amazon. I contacted the TrueVisage Head Office and notified them that I would be returning some products for a refund. I didn't of course mention that some of the boxes had been opened. I knew full well that they would refuse to accept them and there was no way I was going to lose any more money, therefore I immediately set about carefully taping up the boxes to look like they had never been opened. I know this is dishonest, but at the time I thought "fu*k it" – I had lost enough, all TrueVisage had to do was re-box the items. It was my way of giving TrueVisage the proverbial finger. I package everything up and vowed that as soon as the money was back in my account, I would close my TrueVisage account.

There was one last TrueVisage thing I needed to do. I needed to call Cathy, the Gym Owner and apologise. I was happy for Sarah to earn money from Cathy, however I wanted Cathy to be aware of what she was involved in. I owed her that at least. She was a nice person and I didn't want her to be duped as I had been.

I called the gym and Cathy answered. She immediately recognised me and asked how I was. Apparently, Sarah had told her that I had been unwell on the day of the Charity Event, hence my absence. I couldn't help myself and responded saying that Sarah had lied. I was absolutely fine and explained my reason for not attending. I told Cathy to be careful involving herself with TrueVisage. I told her I no longer associated myself with the company as it was all a scam and a pyramid scheme. I apologised saying that I had only recently found out and of course would never had approached her if I had known the truth. I said that I would email the link to the documentary so she could watch it.

I told Cathy that Sarah would now earn commission from all of her purchases and that she should be careful about signing people up to TrueVisage. Cathy reassured me that she was only going to purchase the serums for the Face List Devises, however she would monitor the demand, if it wasn't a popular treatment, then she would stop. She asked if Sarah had given me the money for the device I had sold to her. I laughed at this and briefly explained the situation to Cathy, telling her that Sarah had decided to keep the money for herself. Cathy was shocked and said that she had insisted on paying me by bank transfer, however Sarah had insisted on cash – now I know why. I ended the call to Cathy wishing her all the best and I hoped her gym business continued to prosper. She was a good lady and did a lot for charity. I hoped Sarah wouldn't con her into stocking more products.

All I needed to do now was sort my Spain trip out. I really didn't want to go to the town where the TrueVisage Success Summit was being held. It was a small town and looking online, I saw that it didn't really offer much apart from the beach. I had spoken to James and asked if he could get time off from work so we could perhaps make a little break out of it. He said it was too short notice, I was literally due to fly in less than four days. I also thought about cancelling altogether. I have never travelled on my own and I admit the thought was little daunting.

James said I should try to change the location and treat myself to a stay in a five-star hotel. He told me to use our savings and really splash out, I deserved it after everything I had been through. It was would a chance for me to get some much need "time out". Get away from everyone and really focus on myself. I could then come back after my break, and begin a fresh start and look for a new job. He really is the most amazing husband a woman could wish for. I called

British Airways and asked if I could re-book and decided on Barcelona. I had never been and the city and its sights would keep my mind occupied and hopefully off of TrueVisage. It was done, I was booked into a beautiful hotel, right in the city centre and would spend just over four days on my own. I was so sad that James wouldn't be there with me, however I was secretly looking forward to my own little adventure and some time to simply switch off.

Chapter 40

I thought I had heard the last of TrueVisage on the days leading up to my trip to Barcelona, however it looked like the other girls were just a little too curious as to why I had quit. It wasn't common for a TrueVisage Representative to openly quit the business. You often heard of people "taking a break from it", or taking on another MLM company to represent, such as perfume or health supplements, but actually quitting for good – no way. I had noticed after falling out with Sarah that she, along with all the other so called TrueVisage friends were always monitoring my Instagram feed. As soon as I posted a video on my story, they were the first to view. It was as if they were checking to see if I was posting anything negative about them or TrueVisage.

I had stopped following anyone associated with TrueVisage as I couldn't bear to see anymore bullsh*t posts or product tutorials. It was the same rubbish posted day after day and I felt liberated that I was no longer part of it. However, my life and my posts were of deep interested to them. I found it amusing in a way that they were constantly monitoring my feed. Whilst online one day, I noticed I had received a message. It was from the girl who used to attend the St Albans meetings. She wanted to know how I was – she had heard (obviously) that I had left TrueVisage and wanted to know why. She was blatantly digging and I had a strong suspicion that Sarah had put her up to it.

Part of me wanted to ignore the message. However, there was a chance that she was messaging me off of her own back and if I told her my story, it might convince her to get out. She had been representing TrueVisage for almost 18 months, it might not be too late to save her and convince her to leave.

I messaged back, however I had to be mindful that everything I wrote would no doubt be relayed back to the group, probably read out at one of the meetings, it wouldn't surprise me if my reply was used as an example of a "hater – a Dream Stealer" . I wrote that it was nice of her to contact me and ask how I was. I said that after careful consideration I decided that being partnered with TrueVisage was not for me. I didn't like the person TrueVisage was turning me into. She was obviously online as she replied instantly, asking what I meant. I said that I believed that TrueVisage used cult tactics such as fundamental control, always ingulfing you in *their* activities. They wanted all of your time. You had no time to socialize with anyone non-TrueVisage. All of the mind control was suffocating, the constant push to train you on personal development – the books, videos, tutorials – *you* have to have the right attitude to make it work. If you quit it's your fault. It's all lies designed to make you feel guilty and to pass blame, I was sick of it all.

I told her that as soon as I quit, I immediately started to feel better. I felt like me again. I was happy and stress free and couldn't wait to find a job and get on with my life. I told her she could get out too, that it wasn't too late. I had already been in contact with another two girls who had attended the January Success Summit and had found out with a little bit of coaxing, that they too had quit. There was a delay in her response. I had pushed it too far. She replied back saying that in truth, she was exploring other avenues and wasn't sure if she would continue with TrueVisage. It felt like a small victory, and I was pleased for her. I wished her luck and she asked if she could still follow me on Instagram. I didn't see why not seeing as she was leaving TrueVisage.

My happiness was short lived, as I noticed by looking at her posts that she still went to the Success Summit in Spain, she was super enthusiastic about it and to this day, she still represents TrueVisage. Sadly, another person too brainwashed and too far gone to leave. She had a child and TrueVisage play on this as a way of making women feel guilty if they think about leaving. "Think about your children and their future, you have to go what's best for them and make your business a success" – this is the sort of line spouted at meetings in order to keep mum's hooked. Needless to say, I blocked her as soon as I saw she had lied to me about leaving.

I blocked every single TrueVisage representative still following me on Instagram. I no longer saw the amusement in them following me anymore, I actually thought it was creepy. I wanted nothing more to do with them and their fake friendships.

Epilogue

Walking along the narrow lanes in the old part of Barcelona, I finally felt back to my normal self again. Without the constantly notifications popping up on my phone, the stress of having to continuously post about my life or TrueVisage products – I felt like I had reclaimed my life back. I had booked myself a facial and massage for the last day of my trip and as I lay on the spa bed being massaged, I felt the tension and stresses of the last few months melt away. The trip had been a tonic for my mind, body and soul. I had missed James terribly, however getting away from everyone meant that I could really focus on myself.

I no longer hear from anyone associated with TrueVisage – I had wiped the slate clean and it felt great. I was one of the lucky ones who had managed to break away after only a few months, however I often thought of the people who had been with TrueVisage for years, the brainwashing too deep now for them to escape. It saddens me still to think that so many TrueVisage representatives and other in MLM have broken their relationships with family members and real friends, under the influences of the leaders of TrueVisage and are now at a point where even if they want to leave, they feel that they can't because they have no one else to turn to other that the people involved in the same MLM company.

Multi-Level-Marketing companies are selling a dream, their business practice is based on hope. More than 400, 000 people in the UK are signed up to a MLM company. The majority of those who leave are afraid to speak up. If you leave, people in MLM will say you failed because you didn't try hard enough, not because the business was bad.

If the products were that great and that "amazing" why are they not stocked in shops. Because it's not about the products, it's about recruitment, the product is there to cleverly disguise the cash transaction. If you were simply handing over cash, it would be classed as an official pyramid scheme, which is illegal. The product is the disguise.

MLM's are worth approximately 2 billion in UK. When you effectively have over 100,000 people in the UK doing the same "business" there is no way everyone can make the 4-5 figure monthly salary the company brags you can make as there are simply not enough people to sustain this for everyone. This is why out of say, 1.2 million people around the world working with a MLM company, only approximately 240 people will earn decent money. Not many levels in the pyramid are needed, before you exceed population of the world and that is one of the many reasons why this business is unsustainable.

With TrueVisage, around 89% earned no commission. 1% got about £800 per month, less than minimum wage. 0.04% about 36 people earn good money – 36 people out of thousands. These are the top earners TrueVisage use at events and online to entice you into joining.

This is why we were told to target people with weaknesses, to find a person's "pain". Mine was the fact that I was unhappy with my job, for others it could be financial problems. MLM companies will also target impoverished countries, setting up bases in countries where they know people are desperate to earn money and I am shocked that there are no real regulations in places which monitor how these sort businesses operate.

People involved in cults, people who are brainwashed do not dress differently from you and I. They don't wear a badge; they don't look different. It could be the person sat next to you on the bus, or queuing up to buy a coffee. It was me not long ago and it could easily be someone you know.

In writing this book, I have become part of the rare group of people who are openly speaking out about these companies and how they con people. Most are too embarrassed or afraid of the backlash. If you are involved with a Multi-Level-Marketing company and reading this, and that little shoot of doubt is growing in the pit of your stomach, listen to it. Trust your gut instinct as it will very rarely let you down! My gut told me at the very first meeting that all was not as it seemed, it told me when Sarah said that the speak at the St Albans talk was earning £19,000 a month, but I didn't go with my gut, I ignored it. Do not continue to torture yourself that if you don't buy products to promote, people won't know about the products or your business therefore you won't make money. Do not continue to convince yourself or continue to be brainwashed that you are not doing enough, or that you're doing something wrong as you will get into the vicious cycle of doubt. Do not look on social media and believe what others are posting about how successful their MLM businesses are, 99.9% of the time it's lies and it's fake.

I can hand on heart tell you that by leaving, by stopping what you are doing, you are not quitting. You are not failing at your dreams of being a successful entrepreneur. This is all brainwashing tactics used by the MLM company you are involved in to guilt trip you into continuing. As by staying with them, you are making the company money. This is not about your success and your business, you are making the founders and very, very small percentage of money earning Uplines money. That's it.

You are not a director of your own company because you are partnered with an MLM company. You are not an "international business owner" purely because you signed someone up in another part of the world. Do not let the feelings of embarrassment or the feeling of quitting hold you back, trust me, you will get over it. There is nothing wrong in having a 9-5 job and working for someone else and earning an honest living, just make sure that whatever you do makes you truly happy. Millions, upon Millions of people hold down a normal job – it's how the world works. What would we do if nurses, police, firefighters and all the millions of other people in the world employed to do their 9-5 jobs, which MLM companies tell us to be ashamed to do, decided to quit and work for MLM companies?

Drilling it into you that a "normal" job is bad, is yet another shameful tactic used by MLM company and was used by TrueVisage.

I encourage anyone reading this book and thinking about joining an MLM company or who may well already be with one, to be brave, to leave and reclaim your life. If all of the people you have met within your MLM company are your true friends, they will stick by you – all of my so called TrueVisage friends dropped me as soon as I left. That says it all really. Sarah was family. I haven't heard from her since. Yet, all of my true family and friends have stuck by me and were there when I needed them. Go with your gut instinct and find true happiness.

If my story helps to warn others or helps to encourage people already trapped to leave their MLM company, then I know my move to speak out with this book was not in vain.

2024

I wrote this book back in late 2019, filled it away with the intention of sending out to publishers, then the Covid-19 pandemic brought the world to a standstill and so much more important stuff was happening in the world and in my life, that it was simply forgotten about. Yet my MLM experience never really left me. Being involved with TrueVisage affect me way more than I thought. I buried feelings and if I am being totally honest, the aftershocks of that time still linger with me today. After my trip to Barcelona, I found a job (poorly paid), but one I enjoyed. It was in the hospitality sector and the pandemic hit this industry hard and after almost a year on furlough, I was made redundant. I worked in another two roles and finally settled back in an administrative role. During the pandemic I deleted my Instagram account and no longer had any social media accounts open (although now, due to the publication of this book, I opened an Instagram account dedicated to The Toxic Boss Babe in 2025 as a way of connecting with other like-minded anti-MLM people!). I could see so many MLM's on my feed, taking advantage of the pandemic and post after post about earning money whilst on lockdown. It sickened me. My trust levels are super low, I am wary of so many things, people, charities, businesses. My demeanour has changed also, no longer the open and accepting person I used to be. I continued to practice applying a positivity mindset to life, Covid squashed a bit of it out of me, but a lot of the time, I really found it hard to not force it and even now, I find it difficult to process feelings of anger or sadness, automatically quashing these natural feelings with a positive mindset. Again, I stress that being positive is a good thing – but there is a thing line between honest and pure feelings of happiness and joy and the toxic, forced feelings of positivity.

Recently, I finally accepted that I needed help and am now having telephone therapy sessions. I never really processed what happened to me back in 2019, never really spoke to anyone. Sometimes James and I watch documentaries on Netflix about cults and he comments on how people could be so stupid and a hot rage boil up inside of me. Cults do not target stupid people, on the contrary, they need smart people to pedal the business, they don't want stupid people involved in their "families". He uses TrueVisage as an example which would feel like a rebuke at me for my involvement with them. I don't think he is being deliberately cruel, but I take it the wrong way because unless you have been in my situation, you won't understand. The feeling of shame and foolishness at being duped still hangs over my head, not to mention the money I poured into it all. Anyone I contacted from my list of old friends/contacts etc. I avoid. Perhaps one of the true reasons I came away from social media. I felt fake and no longer found joy in posting about myself and my life. Every time I looked at someone's feed I saw (or believe I saw) something fake, a lie.

I'm working through my feelings now, processing what happened in the hope that one day, I will truly be back to my old self again, but perhaps much wiser and less critical of myself. One day at a time.

If you or anyone you know has been affected by MLM, you can email Linda at: rosalindacarroll27@gmail.com